CHRISTIANS ACCORDING TO THE EPISTLES OF THE NEW TESTAMENT

by

The Rev . Dr. Francis K. Akoa Mongo -

DEDICATION

I dedicate thist book to the late Pasteur Joseph B. Tjéga, my
Director and professor of Systematic Theology at Dager Theological
Seminary in Cameroon. I truly believe that the theological
background I have today comes from his teaching and he was one of
the spiritual people I have known in my life

January 20th, 2014

TABLE OF CONTENTS

THE AUTHOR

François K. Akoa -Mongo is the son of the late Pastor François Akoa Abômô . His nephew Stéphane has named him his exiled uncle who lives in the United States. He was born in Cameroon.

He is the author of 20 books that can be found in Amazon.com . He is the slave of the Lord Jesus whom he serves for the last 47 years . He is the Senior Pastor of a small Congregational Church in Maine for 23 years. He lives in Maine with all his children and his beloved wife, Katherine .

FOREWORD

Whenever I sit down to write a letter, there is always something that drives me to do so. The puropose to write a letter is not only to express your opinion, but also to expect a positive reaction from the receivers or a good outcome of the situation concerned. That means, because of your letter, a positive change or changes have taken place. It is unfortunate that some letters have caused more damage than good. The person who writes or says things which destory others misuses the purpose of letters. As we study letters written by the apostles, we would like to learn about what to expect from a person who has abandoned his or her life of sin, and has been born again in Christ. What kind of person he or she should be according to the 21 letters we have in the New Testament? As the Bible is an inspired Word to guide, rebuke, punish, and shape a man who has become a child of God, what the apostles taught to the Church of the first century is also true today. Putting in a condensed form all these characteristics will do a lot of good for us who live in the 21st century.

My intention in writing this book is to highlight some key lessons that the Christians of the 21st century can easily point the finger at and say " *this is what Paul , Peter, John , Jude, and James teach me that I be a good Christian who expects to receive his crown on the day Christ will return and receive the saint.* "

5

When we read the 21 New Testament epistles, the primary goal of all those who wrote these letters was to give a right direction to the lives of those who had accepted Jesus as their Savior and Redeemer.

The second goal was to prepare them from the coming of the Lord, the parousia. In order to support these two main purposes, there were also some secondary goals:

(1) To protect the purity of the Gospel Message. The apostles knew the true Gospel and they did not want tha Gospel they received from the Lord be altered, polluted by false teachings and those coming from Judaizer Christians. Yes, they have believed in Christ but they misundertood the use of the law of Moses for example. Paul and other apostles rejected their influence. The Law of Moses was their to show us sin, and convict us as being sinners as well as our innability to fulfill the law of God. We are saved by grace when having faith in Jesus who died for us at the cross.;

(2) False teachers, for example those taught that Jesus had already come; or Christians could not be saved by faith alone. These false teachers wanted the believers to believe that faith plus good work, then one can be saved. The apostles insisted that good works should be a proof of our salvation, our how a saved person thanks God for that he has done to him/her. One should not rely on his works for salvation.

6

(3) the third objective was to teach the believers to be able to discern those called anti- Christs. Anti- christ is someone who is a Christian, but his association with other Christians doesn't contribute to the building of their faith. Even though they may look like, speak like and do things like true Chrisitnas, they end up by drawing back those who become their associates to live as pagans. They do not understand the meaning of Christian freedom. Christian freedom is not to live according to the flesh , but to live from from sin in order to glorify and serve the Lord. These Anti-Christ will never openly deny the teachings of the Scriptures, but in practice they live like pagans and cause others to live a life which does please the Lord . The apostles, therefore took the time and to warn good Christians to beware of such Anti- Christs . They put on the skin of a lamb while they are wolves.

(4) The fourth objective in writing these letters concerned persecution. The first century church was the object of persecution. All the apostles died as martyrs, with one exception, John. The apostles taught the saints perseverance. Without that perseverance, we would not have the Bible and the Message of salvation we received. These epistles from the apostles were the root of comfort and strength building up the faith of the persecuted. Persecution was at the same time civic and static.

(5) One of the most important secondary objective of these letters was to build up, strenghten, and let the spiritual growth of the Christians take place in order to reach maturation. The Christians are saved once and for all, but their regeneration and sanctification are progressive. To reach the stature of holiness the Lord expects from those who have receive him is a work which will finish only the day we see Christ face to face as Philippians 2 teaches. Christian continually need spiritual food, advice, exhortations, and recommendations in their daily life when waiting for the coming of the Lord. The 21 epistles are full of constructive and renewal aspects which contribute to growth in faith.

Christians of the 21st century did not solve all the problems. But modeled after the apostles, we can, today, apply the Biblical truth if we rely on the Holy Spirit and the Word of God we have received. One of the great danger in our time is the polluted Gospel our society is trying to convert into true Gospel. There is no authority to condem some teachings as it used to be. Some people were declared heretics, but today, that qualification has no room in our Christian Communities. The Good News suffers confusion in the life of the hearers. Our churches are full of AntiChrists. Churches are persecuted by the immorality of the society. What the apostles prevented happening in the first century can happen in this century of we don't take preventive measures as they did. The question is what is today's church doing to prevent the Great Commission from stopping before the coming of the Lord?

THE MEANING OF BEING SAVED

The term "BEING SAVED" in the Christian tradition carries with it the obvious assumption implying that one is freed from an imminent danger because in the past, his life was in danger. Being saved means someone was on the verge of losing all hope and aspirations; but at this moment, he has hope and aspirations. Being saved according to the Christian faith means having an experience which is true in both parts, that one was saved from something or someone, (Satan and sin) and being saved for something which is (new life and eternal life in God.) When we speak of "salvation" or being saved, these two perspectives should be clear in the experience of the Christian in the Christian tradition.

Being saved implies living a life which is under God guidance and submission. It is self abandonment, self negation as far as desires, pleasures, comfort, importance, ego, and power are concerned. The world and all its values does no longer prevail. But if all the above is what is first, including God, we are living a destructive life which is outside God. When sins such as alcohol, drug abuse and sexual desires, intolerance, lust for power, the pursuit of money at the expense of others, and so on remain at the center of our lives we are far from being saved.

The life of anyone who lives this way seems to be concerned about a need to fill a pit which is bottomless.

But when God is in the center of our lives, we realize that the emphasis on "self " is not a full life. We understand that the "auto-focus" has no future and does nothing to build up someone else or to advance the great causes of this humanity.

But being saved from ourselves means that we are saved to a life that is the exact opposite. That new life is the will of God in which he lets us live. It becomes a priority which is greater than our own will. Being member of the people of God is more important than anything else. It is giving and sharing which is better than taking and accumulating. Our lives become changed by God for the life that affirms others, the life of healing others, a true fulfilling life . Being saved means that we have found wonderful opportunities to share each day with our brothers and sisters and see what God is doing in our lives together. Most people who are saved are beginning to assess their lives, to the point and to find ways to improve who they have become. We believe that salvation is an alarm clock, a call from God to those he has chosen.

PREFACE

Christians of the 21st century in general, and those of Africa in particular, need the knowledge of the power of God and the mystery of his salvation in order to be able to walk in the ways of the Lord .

African Christians as the rest of the believers of the world need to learn more and more how to walk with God. All of us are surrounded if not with ancient beliefs, satanic forces, pagan influence but with Western civilization and culture, the oriental influences, science, philosophy and the great human freedoms trying to suppress Christian religion, it is an imperative duty of those who love the Lord to teach true religion. Our God is a jealous God. There is no room in him with ignoranc and syncretism. Some religious movement leaning toward Pentecotism seem to take over cities and rural even in Africa. These so called churches are now threatening the main Christian institutions all over the world. Protecting and teaching Christians from these influences must become one of the main preoccupations of main stream churches today. This book is put out just for that goal. Our christians need good nourishment for their souls.

Given that there is a great lack in Christian literature of books written by African people, it becomes imperative to counteract these adverse factors that want to bring Africa from where it has always been spiritually. When its time has come for us to take the torch of spiritual world, we promise to do our best and keep our clear minds eager .

I am comforted and would not behave like the prophet Eli who believed to be the only one in Israel who did not worship the Baals. This book is one of those that will enable millions to join me in teaching, educating, training, and leading those who believe in Christ the Redeemer to believe as true Christians who are awaiting for the return of the Savior denouncing everything that is not of Christ. The glory and honor be to Christ our Lord.

INTRODUCTION

The 13 Epistles of Paul have very distinct characteristics. They teach about the respect to Gospel accounts steaming from Christ's crucifixion. Emphasis is put on the joy of the Christian caused by the cross of Jesus Christ, and the life of the believer having his eyes fixed on the new Israel to come.

In those epistles, Paul develops the doctrine of the Church. He sends his letters to the seven churches of the Gentiles plus the letter to the church of Rome which was Jewish. These churches were Rome, Corinth, Galatia, Ephesus, Philippi , Colosse , and Thessalonica. Theese churches learned abou the "mystery which from the beginning of the world, had been hidden in God (Ephesians 3:09) which is now fully revealed. It holds its uniqueness in the councils and the purposes of God. Through Paul alone we know that the Church is not an organization but an organism, the body of Christ, the instinct of his life and heavenly appeal. It lives because of the promise and the purposes of God.

Through Paul alone we know the nature, the purpose, the administrative system of organization of local churches, and right conduct of such gatherings.

It is Paul who taught us that "we shall not all sleep" and that "the dead in Christ shall rise first and the living saints will be "changed" and go to meet the Lord in the air upon Christ's return.

Paul has also developed the doctrines of grace which were latent in the teachings of Jesus Christ. It is he who clearly defines the nature and purpose of the law, the base and the meaning of justification, of sanctification, and of the future glory of the believers, the meaning of Christ's death, the christian position, their work, their expectations, and the service of the Christian in Christ.

It is Paul who developed what is the Church of Jesus Christ on earth, and her blessings. We have been inspired, instructed, and advised through the material covered and strengthened spiritually by learning what I put down in this book. This book is good for the edification of God's people here on earth.

CHAPTER I

WHO WAS PAUL ?

1. PAUL WAS CALLED BY GOD.

Paul simply says, "I went into Arabia." The Orthodox theologian Nicolas Koulomzine considers "this retreat as very significant : Paul follows the royal road of all mystics, he retired to the desert to be alone, to be alone with God . Through this time of reflection, he will feel the Spirit of the Lord totally gripping him. "He discovers the mystery the infinite love of God for the humanity through the rejection of his people and the scandal of the cross."

During this period, continues his spiritual and intellectual transformation that reveals more of Pauline theology. Paul then speaks of his "Gospel": "The gospel I preached is not from a human : it is not from a man that I have received or learned it, but by the revelation of Jesus Christ. "(Gal. 1 : 11-12.)

2 . PAUL WAS A REDEEMED SINNER.

Paul does not hide his past experiance. Luke tells that story clearly concerning the event which took place during Paul's trip to Damascus. The purpose of this trip was to continue what he began in

Jerusalem with the intention to destroy the Christian church still in the form of an egg, the fruit of Jesus' incarnation, death by crucifixion, and his triumph from the dead through his resurrection. If we substract those sad times in history when Paul began by killing Stephen the deacon, we would not have the message of salvation of the world that we have received and continue to preach after so many centuries. Jesus touched the man and he told him that he was not persecuting the church, he persecuted Jesus himself when He appeared to Paul on the road to Damascus, here is what was said: "As he journeyed he came near Damascus, suddenly a light came from heaven flashed around him. He fell to the ground and heard a voice saying : "Saul , Saul, why do you persecute me ?" He replied, "Who are you, Lord," And the Lord said : "I am Jesus , whom you persecuting."(Acts 9 :3- 4).

The word "persecute" in relation to the Church was mentioned for the first time in regard to the church. History shows that all the apostles except John the Elder, were persecuted and died as martyrs. This action did so profound harm to the church that many had to flee from their places. By persecuting Jesus and his church Paul went so far as a leading sinner. Fortunately himself tells the story and admits more than once that he was a sinner; but by the grace of God and his love, he was saved. Jesus did that work on his behalf on the cross.

Paul will no longer be known as a persecutor of the Church, but as a torchbearer of the Gospel among the nations that were far from the promises of the " Old Testament." After his conversion and his new birth in Christ, he became a Christian. He was redeemed by

16

the blood of the Redeemer. Paul himself speaks about his salvation in I Timothy 1: 15 "*This is a faithful saying and worthy of all acceptation, that Christ Jesus came into the world to save sinners, of whom I am chief.* "

The greatest merit of a Christian is to recognize who he was before becoming a Christian, and recognize what the blood of Christ did for him on the cross. If this line between who a person was before the cross and the one he has become remains confused in the life of the saved one, the name of Christian is vainly used. What that person is going to be for the rest of his life will never be different from who he was before calling himself Christian.

The new birth according to Paul based on the Scriptures, is a true spiritual experience we also call "conversion." Through conversion, Paul became a new man living in a dead carcass. In the conversion, there is no change in the outward of the man. The outside stays the same ; no difference from the person before. But from the inside, it is a new creation, a new man. We have a bug in Cameroon which carries with him in the shape of the outer body dead small twigs . We call that bug in Beti " *OBEGE MIMBIM* ", which means " **the one who carries the dead.**" This insect lives and moves with these dead twigs all its life and can't in any way be separated from them. This separation will take place the day insect will die. It is the same for a Christian. He died in his carnal being when he received Christ. He is dead in sin but remains alive in Christ as a spiritual person. Therefore he is strong and renewed in his spiritual side but weak and vulnerable in his carnal side. Saul who persecuted the Church and Jesus himself came out of the house

17

of Ananias in Damascus as a new man with a new name: Paul.

It is wonderful how Paul wanted it to be known for the rest of his life. In history, it is easy to associate the man called Saul with the one who persecuted the Church of Jesus and Paul with the person one who was responsible for evangelizing the pagan world.

The story reminds us of a case that illustrates the same concept Paul had. It concerns the man who was the one who left the funds to create the Nobel Peace Prize. Almost everyone has heard of the Nobel Prize, a collection of awards for achievements in science, medicine, literature and peace. But few people know about the man who created the award and for whom it is named, Alfred Nobel. Alfred Nobel was born in Sweden in 1833. A lively and inquiring mind, combined with a love of science and of chemistry, led him to invent many technological devices all throughout his long life. But he is perhaps best known for his invention of dynamite. Agree to assist in the construction of roads and bridges safely advance, Nobel saw his most famous invention used in the development of military weapons. After a newspaper headline announcing his death by mistake which read "Alfred Nobel, the inventor of dynamite died?" Nobel was inspired to leave another kind of legacy. The man behind the invention of bombs used in war today is best known as the one who established the Nobel Peace Prize. No longer have people remembered him as the inventor of the bombs that kill men. This is the transformation that takes place in the sinner who becomes a believer in Jesus Christ. This happened to Paul as it can happen to anyone who believes.

3. PAUL WAS AN APOSTLE

The Gospels tell us how Jesus chose the twelve Apostles. When Judas hanged himself, in order to choose his replacement, this one was required to meet same conditions than the first ones. He must be a "witness of the resurrection" of Christ, it was necessary that he be selected from those who had "accompanied Jesus during the whole time he walked on the earth" (Acts.1:2 -22). If Paul had to be selected on this basis, he would never be an apostle. The passage of II Corinthians 12 :1 -5 where Paul speaks of a supernatural experience that happened to him before the beginning of his ministry, although he did not want to talk about it, let us think about God who revealed the Gospel to him. Was this the period that revelation took place? No one knows. But from that point, Paul vehemently defends his apostleship throughout his epistles. For this reason, Paul became the thirteenth apostles. Paul naturally distinguishes his own case from that of "those who were apostles before" him (Gal. 1: 17). He recognizes their special place in the life of the Church. And yet, as everyone knows, Paul had his own way to interpreted the Gospel as an apostle in the strict sense. It is certain that, in the first century, at the origin of the Church, no one else traveled as many miles as Paul on land and sea for the sole purpose of proclaiming the Gospel. So he had an apostolic concept that went beyond what other Twelve had in mind. The book of Acts shows that Acts (Acts 1,2.26 , 6 , 2).

Indeed, in the First Letter to the Corinthians Paul makes a clear

19

distinction between "the Twelve" and himself. One may even see that in his mind, there were two groups of apostles: the twelve who were called by Jesus on this earth in one hand, and himself in the other (cf. 15, 5.7). That is why in the same text, he then humbly called himself as **"the least of the apostles,"** even comparing himself to a runt and saying verbatim: "I am not worthy to be called an apostle, because I persecuted the Church of God. But what I am, I am by the grace of God and the grace which he has bestowed upon me was not in vain I gave worth more than all the others. Actually it's not me; it is the grace of God within me "(1 Cor 15: 9-10). The metaphor of "**the runt"** expresses extreme modesty. "I am the last of all, I'm a freak. This is what God does in a person who, from the evangelical point of view, could be considered a waste! But because of the blood of Jesus, he is now worthy.

Paul's letters define his apostleship in three ways... The first Paul was an apostle because he has "seen the Lord" (1 Cor 9: 1) , that is to say has had a decisive encounter with him in his life . Similarly, in the Letter to the Galatians (1 : 15-16) he said that he was called , almost selected by the grace of God and the revelation of his Son for the glad tidings to the Gentiles. Ultimately, it is the Lord who called anyone to the apostolate , not one own presumption. An apostle does not just happen to be; it happens by the choice of the Lord. It is not for nothing that Paul says he is " apostle" (Romans 1, 1) , that is to say "sent not from men nor by human means , but by Jesus Christ and God the Father "(Gal 1, 1.) This is the first characteristic of Paul's apostleship : He saw and was called by the Lord.

The second feature was "having been sent." The Greek word means for apostle is " apostolos " meaning sent, mandated " that is to say, ambassador and bearer of a message. That person must be responsible and a representative of the one who sends him. This was the reason Paul called himself " an apostle of Christ Jesus" (1 Cor 1: 1 , 2 Cor 1 1) , that is to say, his delegate, placed entirely at his service , also called "servant of Jesus Christ" (Romans 1: 1). This principle appears in the foreground idea of someone else initiative that is God in Christ Jesus that we owe a full obedience, but he particularly emphasized that we have received from God a mission in his name.

The third characteristic was years of the "proclamation of the Gospel," with the consequent the foundation of many churches. In fact, the title " apostle " was not and could not be an honorary title. It involved concretely and even dramatically throughout the existence of the subject concerned. In the First Letter to the Corinthians, Paul exclaims: "Am I not an apostle? Have I not seen Jesus our Lord? Are you not the result of my work in the Lord? Even though I may not be an apostle to others, surely I am to you. For you are the seal of my apostleship in the Lord"." (9: 1-2) . Similarly, in the Second Letter to the Corinthians he says : " It is you yourselves are our letter, written on our hearts, known and read by everybody." (3, 2-3). Paul was totally convinced of his calling as an apostle.

4 . GOD GAVE THE GOSPEL TO PAUL

Oh ! If you could bear with me a little crazy ! But you bear with me ! For I am jealous over you with godly jealousy, for I have espoused you to one husband, to present you as a chaste virgin to Christ. " 2 Corinthians 11: 1"

Monitor Paul's thought here through his words and phrases used; it seems that he considered the Corinthian believers as wives and Jesus the bridegroom that the Gospel he brought to this community believers has made him the priest who celebrated the marriage between them and Jesus. He also speaks of "the jealousy of God."The kind of jealousy that God expresses when human beings who belong to him worship another god; it was a such jealousy that Paul felt as he did not want the Corinthians to observe any other teaching except the Gospel himself brought to them in order to receive salvation"

Paul was an apostle who was devoted to the Gospel of the kingdom to the point that he might have feelings for God himself. This is the depth of the spirituality of Paul which allowed him to define the contours of the Church of Jesus Christ not only on doctrinal points, but also in the physical organization and the qualifications of those who teach should be as models and spiritual leaders of the Church. He himself always shared those qualities and was able to find solutions to all spiritual problems that arose in spiritual communities throughout his epistles .

What is said about Paul is also true about the other apostles, who were authors of the Epistles which are in the New Testament. Paul was a spiritual leader who first established a strong and deep spiritual relationship with God, which changed his heart, his eyes, his feelings, his thoughts according to the Holy Spirit so that he could lead God's church through positive contributions. What about us in the 21st century?

What Paul said in the first century is true today, we should not let any other preaches another Jesus than the one Paul preached, or receive another spirit, than the one we have received, or another Gospel than the one we have accepted. (2 Corinthians 11:5)

The Gospel Paul received and brought to the believers of his time was so complete, so pure, and so true that any other gospel, even if Paul or another apostle or an angel were to change or add something, this one would have been anathema.

For the first time this term was used in the New Testament. The apostle John also used it in the book of Revelation 22: 19. Therefore to study and to understand Paul means you have learned from a great teacher of the Gospel of the Kingdom of God as well as all that man should know and practice to be a member of God's family.

5 . PAUL SUFFERED MORE THAN OTHERS

Here is in what sense Paul believes that he has contributed more than the other apostles for the advancement of the Gospel and the Kingdom of God. He writes in 2 Corinthians 11 :23 -31, "Are they servants of Christ? (I am out of my mind to talk like this.) I am more. I have worked much harder, been in prison more frequently, been flogged more severely, and been exposed to death again and again. Five times I received from the Jews the forty lashes minus one. [25] Three times I was beaten with rods, once I was pelted with stones, three times I was shipwrecked, I spent a night and a day in the open sea, I have been constantly on the move. I have been in danger from rivers, in danger from bandits, in danger from my fellow Jews, in danger from Gentiles; in danger in the city, in danger in the country, in danger at sea; and in danger from false believers. I have labored and toiled and have often gone without sleep; I have known hunger and thirst and have often gone without food; I have been cold and naked. Besides everything else, I face daily the pressure of my concern for all the churches. Who is weak, and I do not feel weak? Who is led into sin, and I do not inwardly burn? If I must boast, I will boast of the things that show my weakness. The God and Father of the Lord Jesus, who is to be praised forever, knows that I am not lying....

6 . HE BELIEVED TO HAVE THE PURE GOSPEL

Listen to Paul, " I marvel that you are so soon removed from him that called you into the grace of Christ, to a different gospel . Not that there is another gospel, but there are some that trouble you , and would pervert the gospel of Christ. But though we , or an angel from heaven, preach any other gospel than that which we have preached unto you , let him be anathema !" (Galatians 1 :6 -8)
Christ preached the Gospel! But what is it? Did the apostle Paul preached the same gospel to the Gentiles ? According to what he said here, it was the same Gospel that he preached to the Gentiles. Christ taught, "Repent, and believe in the Gospel" (Mark 1: 15). But what was the true gospel ? And is there more than one? The answer to these questions, and many others, are in the Bible. And their understanding is very ESSENTIAL to us. However , they remained

hidden from the vast majority of so-called Christians .

Six new religious books are published each day in the United States - in addition, there are more than two thousand different religions! Yet there never was so much confusions and conflicts among the pseudo-Christians or the world in general, about the real answers to life's problems. Why ? How is it then that knowledge is so prolific that there is , at the same time , so much ignorance of the truth about the BIG QUESTIONS OF LIFE ? Are answers to these questions have something to do with the Gospel?

7 . SMALL BUT STRONG IN CHRIST.

Paul knew that being in Christ is to let the Spirit and Christ fight for you. Paul did not fight against his enemies or against his old man, or with the world, or with Satan and his agents. He left the enamored and divine strength to fight for him. That is why he emphasized and recognized his death in the flesh, dead in his desires, dead in sin but alive in the Spirit and in Christ. Nowhere in his letters could Paul see himself acting in the flesh. Sometimes he took those who had known him as witnesses of his fidelity to Christ," For you yourselves know how you ought to imitate us , because we did spot ducts wanton among you" (II Thess.3: 7) II Thess.3: 7 "For you yourselves know how you ought to follow our example, because we did not act in an undisciplined manner among you. Paul knew that his strength came from God , " I can do all things through Christ who strengthens me (Phil. 4: 13). Paul himself says, "If I wanted to boast, I would not be a fool , because I say the truth : but I forbear, lest any man should think of me a higher opinion that he sees in me or what it means to me. And lest I should be exalted above, because of the abundance of the revelations, there was given me a thorn in the flesh, a messenger of Satan to buffet me and keep me from exalting myself. Three times I pleaded with the Lord depart from me, 9 and he said to me: My grace is sufficient for you, for my power is made perfect in weakness . Therefore I will boast all the more gladly of my weaknesses, that the power of Christ may rest upon me"(2 Corinthians 12: 6-9). Paul totally relied in God, in the Spirit and in Jesus in all his life and his ministry.

8 . A MODEL FOR OTHER CHRISTIANS

When one studies the life of Paul, he will see that he was a Christian who had never denied that he was a sinner, and indeed he was considered the worst from all the blood of Christ has saved. Here's what he said about in I Timothy 1: 15 "This is a faithful saying and worthy of being fully received : Christ Jesus came into the world to save sinners, of whom I am chief." He was also very convinced about who he had become, because of Christ his Lord and Savior. Here is how he described the person he was in Galatians 2: 20 "I have been crucified with Christ and it is no longer I who live, but Christ who lives in me; and I now live in the flesh I live by faith , faith in the son of God, who loved me and gave himself up for me." That is why he described what he did throughout his lives before meeting his Lord face to face in these terms, Philippians 3: 13 "But one thing I do, forgetting those things which are behind and reaching forth to those that are before, I press the goal for the prize of the heavenly call of God in Christ Jesus. "

Paul was the only one in the Bible who could tell those he brought to God through the Good News, " Be imitators of me, as I myself am of Christ" (1 Corinthians 11:1)

Paul also said to Christians, "Imitate God" (Ephesians 5: 1 and at the same time that he said to them "Imitate me as I imitate Christ" (I Corinthians 4: 16 , I Thessalonians 1 . 6 2 Thessalonians 3 : 7; Hebrews 13: . . 7). Imitation is possible only in a specific contact, perfect knowledge , monitoring in relationships. It is in this context that Jesus told his disciples in John . 14: 9 "Whoever has seen me has seen the Father. "

Can mimicking other people , for example influential Christians, is what Paul is saying here. However, there is no way to avoid what is said in Ephesians 5:1 : "Become imitators of God."   Paul could tell other Christians to imitate him because he was 100% Imitator of God. He was 100% sure that he was a good imitator of Jesus Christ. It was for this reason loved using the word "imitator" in several passages throughout his epistles.

Here is what Paul meant by the word –to imitate "to strive to be like" The Greek word " *mimétès,* " which literally means " imitator." Greeks, this may be in large part what the poets or actors, comedians "on bad terms" or charlatan do. Mimeomaï the verb, which means to imitate , or in the physical sense (voice , gestures, cries ...), or the moral sense (stock, quality), ... appears in 2 Thessalonians 3:7 and 9 (imitate the apostle) Hebrews 13:7 (imitating spiritual leaders) and 3 John 11 (imitate the good.)

Paul knew perfectly well that he had lived a true Christian life. That is why he said this at the end of his days, "*I have fought the good fight , I have finished the race, I have kept the faith . Now the crown of righteousness is reserved for me the Lord, the righteous judge, shall give me at that day , and not to me only , but unto all them also that love his appearing*. (II Timothy 4:7-8).

9 . MANY FALSE TEACHERS

Some Christians believe that the Gospel does not relate only to the person of Christ. Believing in the person of Jesus Christ in order to have eternal life, is what the Bible teasches us. But others have associated the Gospel with or made these secondary phases so important that the true Gospel was lost and became less important. Some preach the gospel of miracles, the gospel of music, the social gospel, the popular gospel, the money gospel, the personality gospel. This is wrong. When we don't let Jesus be in the center, that means we believe in a different Gospel than the one preached by Paul and found in the Bible.

Note again the story of Mark: " After John was put in prison , Jesus came into Galilee , preaching the gospel of God" (v. 14) . This sentence covers the whole work of Jesus in Galilee. We can therefore establish the contours of the Gospel of God here. And it was in this context that He said, "Repent, and BELIEVE IN THE GOOD NEWS [THE GOSPEL] ." What Gospel? The Gospel of the "Kingdom of God" . Marc alluded to this message by saying in verse 1: "The beginning of the gospel of Jesus Christ." The Gospel of Christ relates THE KINGDOM OF GOD - and nothing else! We must believe in the Gospel, and not a substitute or counterfeit. It is the gospel of God which encompasses the entire life saved. It is the Gospel which is the Kingdom of God on earth. It is the gospel that recrutes members of the Kingdom of God on earth.

10 . DEFENDANT OF THE GOSPEL

This topic is so important that God inspired the Apostle Paul to give this warning to the Galatians and to us today: "*I marvel that you are so soon removed from him that called you into the grace of Christ, to move to another gospel. Not that there is another gospel, but there are some that trouble you , and would pervert the gospel of Christ. But though we , or an angel from heaven, preach any other gospel than that which we have preached unto you , let him be anathema ! We have said before, I say again , if anyone preaches any other gospel to you than that ye have received, let him be anathema!*" (Gal. 1 :6 -9)

The question we might ask is whether the gospel that Paul preached was different from the other apostles. It is clear that at the Jerusalem conference, Paul and Barnabas were recognized as bearers of the Gospel to the Gentiles. Throughout the ministry of Paul and his helpers , some false teachers Paul gave the name "Judaizing " sought to infiltrate the Christian communities founded by Paul, then later addressed his epistles. By studying the Epistles of Peter, Jude, of James , Titus and John, same trouble makers were also named and dismissed in their epistles. Therefore , Paul, Peter, Jude, James , Titus and John preached the same Gospel. If the Paul and the auther apostles opposed the same false teachers, that means the Gospel preached by Paul was identical to the Gospel preached by all other apostles.

Paul believed that God entrusted him with the true Gospel . Here is what he said, "God judged us worthy of our trust with the gospel , so we speak, not as pleasing to men , but to please God who tests our hearts. " (I Thessalonians 2: 4). This responsibility was not taken lightly by Paul . True ministers always teach what God commands , not what pleases men.

(including " scholars " of the Bible). Therefore, no one could prove to Paul his teaching was not the true Gospel. He kept saying that he did not learn or receive his Gospel from men but from God.

11 . WHAT IS THE GOSPEL ?

The word "gospel " means " good news." The expression "kingdom of God " , simply means the government of God. Therefore Christ preached "the good news of God's government." Later in this book, we will see where, when, what, how, and why the Good News, and how it relates to what is undoubtedly the greatest prophecy of all time.)

The theme of the GOSPEL OF THE KINGDOM OF GOD is not only dominant in the New Testament, but IS THE WHOLE BIBLE. And yet , most people hardly know anything about it , if anything at all. Pastors and ministers of churches ignore this gospel of the Son they never preach. The world is virtually ignorant of this great truth . And all those who know MUST CORRECTLY PREACH IT. THIS

IS INDEED THE PURPOSE OF THIS BOOK: THE TEACHING
OF THE KINGDOM OF GOD.

12 . ALL THE APOSTLES PREACHED THAT GOSPEL

Can we prove that the New Testament writers also preached the
same gospel? Absolutely! The Apostle Paul preached to the Gentiles
(heathen) . (Acts 19 : 8) says, " And having entered the synagogue
and spoke boldly for three months discoursing and persuading the
things of the kingdom of God. " In several places in his epistles Paul
taught at various Christian communities made up of Gentiles . His
message was always the same. He constantly preached, taught and
referred to the Kingdom of God.

The apostle Peter also preached about the Kingdom: "For so an
entrance shall be ministered unto you abundantly into the everlasting
kingdom of our Lord and Savior Jesus Christ." (II Pet 1: 11).

The apostle James did the same : " Hearken, my beloved brethren :
God did not chosen the poor of this world to be rich in faith and
heirs of the kingdom that he has promised to those who love him? "(
James 2: 5).

On three different occasions Matthew used the phrase "the Good
News of the kingdom." Here is an example: "Jesus went about all the
cities and villages , teaching in their synagogues, preaching the good
news of the kingdom, and healing every disease and every infirmity"
(9: 35).

In almost each of His parables, Christ taught the essentials of the

Kingdom of God. Matthew alone refers to the Kingdom of God more than fifty times.

Luke says that Christ commissioned His disciples to preach the same message: "Jesus called the twelve ... He sent them to preach the kingdom of God" (9 :1 -2). Later a little more, Christ appointed seventy others to go and preach the same message of the Kingdom of God (9 : 1, 9).

The kingdom of God relates to the daily life of the one who believes in Jesus Christ. Its expectation concerns the return of Christ. Therefore, a member of that kingdom lives in the presence and in the service of God when waiting for Jesus' return. Therefore, any action, every thought, every relationship and the Christian behavior must be imbued with the will of God and guided by the Holy Spirit. The human factor must be removed in any moment of one who belongs to the kingdom of God. This is the gospel that Paul and the other apostles were instructed and preached in the New Testament.

13 . THE MISSION OF THE HEATHEN

The missionary commitment of Paul might have started in the Christian community of Antioch where he was the host. (Acts 15: 22) " Then the apostles and elders within the whole church thought that it was proper to send a delegation of Jerusalem made up of Paul and Barnabas It was at the Council of Jerusalem that this decision of their mission to proclaim the Good News of Jesus to the Gentiles was made. Luke says in Acts," Barnabas and Saul, sent by the Holy Spirit, went down to Seleucia , and from there they sailed to Cyprus.

Arrived at Salamis, they preached the Word of God in the synagogues of the Jews ... ". Here, there is even mention of the Holy Spirit in choosing (Acts 13 :1 -4) This holy partnership with the Holy Spirit will work in Paul . That choice of Paul might have made him aware of his responsibilities and also moved him into action .

During the first mission in Asia Minor , through Cyprus, the good news was announced in smaller centers such Paphos, Perga , Pisidian Antioch , Iconium, Lystra and Derbe . Barnabas was first the executive head of this mission. When Paul took command in successive missions, he begun to act methodically.   Look the kind of choices he made for Christian communities he founded in strategic cities according to the geographic , economic and cultural field.s All these cities were centers of radiation as provincial capitals of the empire.

Christian communities founded by Paul were strong in faith and became missionary centers, to spread the faith in the nearest towns . Paul was quick to organize the Church. Antioch from which Barnabas and Paul have made their first trip served as a model. And the message was spread to Philippi , Thessalonica , capital of the province of Macedonia, Corinth , the capital of the province of Achaia, and Ephesus , and finally Athens .
Paul went to bring the good news to the Galatians .

Luke throughout the book of Acts revealed the history of salvation, which was to go all the way to Rome. In fact Rome did not know Paul apostolic activity. In fact Rome already had a thriving Christian church when Paul wrote a letter to them. When Paul wrote from Corinthian a letter to the Christian community of Rome, he did so only to announce his missionary journey to Spain and its passing through Rome. The proposed stay was only one step and not for evangelism . Shortly, before the planned trip took place, Paul was arrested in Jerusalem and his journey did not actually occurre.

Some reports had reached Paul whereby foreign missionaries attacked his gospel . As Paul did not intervene in other communities founded by others, he did not accept foreign interference in his communauties. The gospel he announced was received from God himself.

Difficulties of all sorts had arisen in Galatia , Corinth and Ephesus . It was during this difficult time that Paul wrote his letters to Christians communauties of these cities.

A letter written from Corinth to the Christian communauties of Rome shaped the themes of the Gospel Paul was spreading in the eastern part of the empire. Paul addressed the burning issues of faith. We know his intention to proclaim the Gospel to the limits of the Western world (Rom 15.24 to 28) .

Paul chose the highly skilled Christians to be in charge of all Christian communauties he founded.   He specified the expectations he had for each one and each groups of certain responsibilities. Timothy for exemple, here is what he recommaded him to do, "Be the model of the believers, in word , in conduct, in love, in faith , in purity. Until I come, attach yourself to read, to exhortat, to teach. Be careful ... to yourself a... "((1 Timothy 4 :12- 13, 16). It would be the same for deacons, elders, and even Christian members. High

33

expectations was Paul's way of life as servant and believer in Christ.

CHAPTER II

PAUL'S BELIEFS

Introduction: There are those who speak of the " Paulinian Theology" , I call it the core beliefs of Paul or even Paul's thought process . Each of us has a theology , some convictions, a universe in which we operate mentally and from which we conceive ideas and mobilize ourselves for concrete actions. I remember when I was a student in theology, one of my classmate and friend, Samuel AKONO ELA; he used to say that his God was an old man sitted on the throne with a long white beard. Ifsomeone would remove that image of God being that way in his understanding of who God is, there would be no God Savior at all for him to give his life to.

What I would like to do in this chapter is to develop what we believe to be the core beliefs that made Paul the one we know through his 13 epistles and although in the pan of his doctor , the author of Luke Gospel.

1 . HIS GOSPEL FROM GOD.

When we read the Epistles of Paul , one of its signatures at the beginning of these letters was, " Paul, a servant of Jesus, called to be an apostle , " set apart for the Gospel of God "(Rom.1 : 1) He would also add other phrases as in I Corinthians 1: 1 ,and in II Corinthians 1: 1 " by the will of God.". He used the same phrase in Ephesians 1: 1 , Colossians 1 : 1, II Timothy 1: 1.

In Galatians 1 : 1, he said, " Paul, an apostle not from men , neither by man , but by Jesus Christ and God the Father who raised him from the dead." In I Timothy 1 : 1, he said, " by the command of God our Father and Jesus Christ our hope."

If the idea of being called by God for a spécific task and in a different way was not so important for Paul, he would not have repeated that at least seven times when writing these 13 letters to different churches and individuals.

Paul wanted everyone to know that his calling among people who had the name of "apostles" was higher compared to the other apostles, because it was done according to the " **will of God**" , "**by God" "coming from God**". The will of God and nothing else that God's will was the reason Paul was in the ministry and in charge of this specific mission: to preach the Good News to the Gentiles..

The Paul setting aside , not by a man, but by Jesus Christ and God our Father " placed Paul in a different level than the other apostles. When Paul writes this words, one can see him in his encounter with Jesus on the road to Damascus in Chapter 9 of Acts. The resurrected and ascended Jesus came from heaven in order to appeared to him . The echo of that encounter in Acts is heard here in Galatians 1: 15 "But when it pleased God, who separated me from my mother 's womb and called me by his grace, to reveal his Son in me so that I might preach him among the Gentiles , so early, I conferred not with flesh and blood ... ". One can see that Paul saw himself throughout his ministry as a New Testament Jeremiah . His calling and Jeremiah calling from the weomb of his mother become alike. Paul's words in Galatians are identical to those prounounde by God to Jeremiah 1: 5 " " Before I formed you in the womb I knew you . Before you were born , I chose you to serve me. I made you my spokesperson of the people. " Paul is telling the Christians of the first century as to us that he was called for a specific mission and he took that mission very seriousely.

In the same chapter of Galatians , Paul speaks of something that remains a mystery. He says in 1 :17 -24 " *I conferred not with flesh and blood , neither went I up to Jerusalem to them which were apostles before me , but I went into Arabia , and returned again to Damascus Then three years after I went up to Jerusalem to get acquainted with Peter and stayed with him fifteen days . , and I saw none of the other apostles , safe the brother James, the Lord's brother. Now the things which I write unto you, behold before God I do not lie Then I went into the regions of Syria and Cilicia and I was unknown by face to the assemblies of Judea that are in Christ, but they had heard only . that he who persecuted us past, now preaches the faith he once destroyed , and they glorified God because of me*" (v. 18-24) .

This last passage clearly shows that Paul had had no contact to learn the message he brought to the Gentiles from man . It clarifies his contacts with "those who were apostles before him." It shows that these contacts were for some specific objectives not regarding the learning content of the Gospel. Paul did not have any contact for getting information or going to school. However, we remember that Jesus spent three years with his disciples during which they learn the Gospel the later on preached.

Here's something else that Paul said about his Gospel in Galatians 1 :11 -12, " But I certify you , brethren, that the gospel which was preached by me is not according to man . For I have not received it of man , neither was learned, but by the revelation of Jesus Christ. " The Gospel is not ACCORDING MAN, but BY THE REVELATION OF JESUS CHRIST".

When Paul was converted to Christianity, Jesus was already in heaven . What happened in " Arabia" fourteen years between the time Paul met Jesus on the road to Damascus and the beginning of his ministry in the regions of Syria and Cilicia remains a mystry. Paul himself did not elaborate on it.

From this passage, we have no doubt that in the mind of Paul , his Gospel was different from that of the apostles. The main difference we see is the interpretation of the place of the Law of Moses in the life of the believers. Paul and other apostles disagreed on this point. For Paul, a sinner is saved by grace and faith in Jesus Christ. We will discuss this issu concerning the Law of Moses later on.

2 . THE PREVAILING GOSPEL

When we read the book of Acts of the Holy Spirit , there was a Christian church in Jerusalem that James was the head . Paul and

Barnabas were appointed by the Council of Jerusalem to be the bearers of the Good News to the Gentiles while the other Apostles would continue with the Jews. Throughout the ministry of Paul , he was fighting against the Judaizers . Some identified them as Jewish Christians who wanted to influence the Gentiles who become Christians to be circumcised, to observe days of the week , to follow Jewish traditions, to observe the Law of Moses , not to eat some meat and many other things coming from Judaïsm. The group as many called them the Judeo- Christian teaching is summarized in Acts 15.1: " Some men came down from Judaea taught the brethren , and said : "If you do not get circumcised according to the custom of Moses, you can not be saved (even if you have accepted Jesus as Savior Messiah) . "

Subjects going along with these things brought the difference between Paul - Barnabas and the other apostles whose alligiance was tied to Jerusalem .

The proposition Peter made during the Jerusalem Councile reinforced and affirmed Paul's position in his ministry among the Gentiles , " Now then, why do you try to test God by putting on the necks of Gentiles a yoke that neither we nor our ancestors have been able to bear? [11] No! We believe it is through the grace of our Lord Jesus that we are saved, just as they are" (Acts 15.10-11) .

Acxcording to the history, the Judeo-Christian position did not prevail and the Christian Church was built on the Paulian Theology. Towards the end, as we see in all the epistles, there were no discrepancies in the doctrinal positions going against Paul, and the other epistles do not reinforce the Judeo-position the Christian communauty of Jerusalem had before.

3 . GRACE , JUSTIFICATION , FAITH

Paul understood some passages of the Gospels , for example, John 3:
16 "For God so loved the world that he gave his only begotten Son,
that whosoever believes in him should not perish , but have
everlasting life".
The message Peter gave the day of Pentecost ," Delieve in the Lord
Jesus and you will be saved".

Also in Jon 10:9 " I (Jesus) I am the door : by me if any man enter in
, he shall be saved, and shall go in and out, and find pasture ". (John
10:9). Jesus said unto him, " I am the way and the truth and the life :
no man comes to the Father but by me" . (John 14: 6).

"And the last day, that great day of the feast, Jesus stood and cried ,
saying, If anyone thirsts, let him come to Me and drink (John 7: 37)

"And ... there is salvation in any other: for there is none other name
under heaven given among men by which we must be saved. (Acts 4
: 12)

" All have sinned and fall short of the glory of God "(Ro. 3 : 23)

But God has a remedy . Jesus Christ died on the cross and paid the penalty for our sins. If you repent , if you confess your sins and if you ask Jesus to be your Lord and Savior, He will forgive you , instead of being condemned , you have eternal life . The time is fulfilled , and the kingdom of God is at hand : repent you , and believe the gospel.". (Mark 1: 15)

" Whoever believes in Him is justified , that is to say that we are the estimated righteous before God, righteous faith in Christ , because He who knew no sin, God " was made sin for us , so that we might become the righteousness of God in him " (2 Cor. 5:21) .

The justification exeeds the purification of guilt, or the forgiveness of sins , because we have a positive righteousness coming from Jesus who has made us clean in the eyes and the presence of God. The blood of Christ , as we have seen, is the meritorious cause , worth so infinite in our favor, that glorified and atoned our sins. God justly did justice on his Son, so that we receive , forgive, justification, and restauration by the same act of Christ on the cross. As the apostle expresses it elsewhere : "It is because of him that you are in Christ Jesus, who has become for us wisdom from God—that is, our righteousness, holiness and redemption" (1 Cor 1:30.) .

We are so completely identified with Christ before God, that place is our place, accepting our acceptance , because we are in Him , that is why the apostle John could write : " This is how love is made complete among us so that we will have confidence on the day of judgment: In this world we are like Jesus " (1 John 4:17) . This will suffice to show the completeness of our justification, and to help souls anxious to understand that it is God Himself who justifies the believer.

4 . SAVED BY GRACE

The French philosopher Blaise Pascal said: " To make a man a saint, grace is absolutely necessary and anyone who doubts this , does not know what a saint or what a man is. "

Paul was a true Pharisee who knew and lived according to the Law of Moses. He studied the gospel of Jesus Christ and came to the conclusion that only the faith in God's grace is the only means by which a sinner , a man born in sin can receive eternal life .

Normally, no man outside Jesus can save us. It is impossible for man to save himself . Salvation is a gift from God. The only way by which man can obtain salvation is only through God's plan . The good news is that the road was opened by Jesus. Consciously or unconsciously, every man seeks and need salvation and the door is found only in Jesus Christ.

There are those who believe and say we should do this or that to be saved. For Christians , salvation is primarily a gift, and is obtained by grace, unmerited favor . Faith in itself does not save : it is the means by which man appropriates the work of Christ on the cross

42

which saves.

Grace is grace in Jesus Christ. It is based on the atoning work of Jesus Christ. Out of the cross no grace. Jesus had to die on the cross so that grace be offered . It is Jesus who paid the price that saved us .

If man does not knows at Jesus' door, it remains lost . The man can do good works and these works are good in the eyes of God because he is saved. Works in themselves can not save us. Anyone who believes he can be saved by his works, not only that he is wrong , but also he remains in his sins . It is with faith in the work done by Jesus Christ, his death on the cross that we are saved. The following biblical passages from the apostles' letters will confirm this truth :

Ephesians 2: 8-9. For it is by grace you have been saved, through faith—and this is not from yourselves, it is the gift of God— [9] not by works, so that no one can boast.

Romans 3: 10, 20 and 23-28 . As it is written : There is none righteous , not even one ; no flesh will be justified in his sight by works of the law, since through the law comes the knowledge of sin . for all have sinned and fall short of the glory of God, and all are justified freely by his grace through the redemption that came by Christ Jesus. God presented Christ as a sacrifice of atonement, through the shedding of his blood—to be received by faith. He did this to demonstrate his righteousness, because in his forbearance he had left the sins committed beforehand unpunished— he did it to demonstrate his righteousness at the present time, so as to be just and the one who justifies those who have faith in Jesus.

Where, then, is boasting? It is excluded. Because of what law? The law that requires works? No, because of the law that requires faith. For we maintain that a person is justified by faith apart from the works of the law ».

Galatians 3 :10. For all those who are of the works of the law are under the curse: for it is written, Cursed is everyone who does not abide by all things written in the book of the law , and not a doer .

1 Timothy 2 :3-4. For this is good and acceptable in the sight of God our Savior; Who will have all men to be saved, and to come unto the knowledge of the truth.

CHAPTER III

PAUL'S GOSPEL

1 . THE GOSPEL OF PAUL : BEFORE AND AFTER

Paul believes that being a Christian means having in life a demarcation line between the period before and the period after one have received Jesus as Savior and Redeemer. He abandon a certain identity and receive or develop another . If a Jew or a nice you were , you become another person different from the first . So you can not be both Jewish and Christian , kind and Christian , Cameroon and Christian. The Christian is someone other than the Jew, the Gentile , African , American or European etc. ....

Gal.2 : 20 " I have been crucified with Christ, nevertheless I live , it is no longer I who live, but Christ lives in me , I now live in the flesh I live by faith in the Son God , who loved me and gave himself up for me ..

Gal.3 : 38 I am crucified with Christ, and I live , no longer I, but Christ lives in me . God forbid that I should glory in anything save in the cross of our Lord Jesus Christ, by whom the world is crucified to me , and I am crucified to the world . "

"Knowing that our old man was crucified with him." (Rom. 6:6) .

"Those who are Christ's have crucified the flesh." (Gal. 5: 34).

1 Corinthians 24:13 We all have , indeed, been baptized by one Spirit into one body, whether Jews or Greeks, whether slaves or free , and we were all made to drink of one Spirit . "

It is very important to understand this truth and proclaim aloud and live in reality. "If by the Spirit you mortify the deeds of the body , ye shall live ." (Rom. 8: 18).

Paul advises Christians to death the earthly man (Col. 8:5). So according to him , the man , the person who bears the name of Christian is the heavenly man . He no longer lives in the flesh but in the Spirit , because Christ lives in him . (Rom. 7: 18).

The phrase " born again" literally means " born from above ." Nicodemus had a real need. He needed a change of heart - a spiritual transformation. The new birth , being " born again " is an act of God whereby eternal life is given to the person who believes (2 Corinthians 5:17 , Titus 3:5 , 1 Peter 1:3 , 1 John 2:29 , 3:9 , 4:7 ; 5:1-4,18) .

46

Paul speaks of two Adams to mean both creations ". That is why it is written, "The first man Adam became a living soul . The last Adam was made a quickening spirit . The first man is of the earth , earthy : the second man is from heaven . " 1 Corinthians 15:45,47 . Those who are born of the Spirit , those who are born again , those who are Christians are born in the second Adam who is Christ

God entrusted the earth and what is there to Adam and Eve (Genesis 1:28) , they were free and they were not to know death , because they ate the fruit of the tree of life , and sinned by disobeying the one commandment that God gave them. From that moment Adam and Eve lost their communion with God and they became mortal (Genesis 3:19) . We all human beings are descendants of Adam and Eve; therefore, we inherited their mortal , sinful nature .

Jesus came to restore all things , he came to repair the fault of all mankind ; he came to collect the keys of Hades; he came to conquer death through His sacrifice on the cross; he came to reconcile us with God. Christian has gone through a new creation in Christ Jesus. This concept is very important for Paul in particular. The old Adam in the Christians is dead and the new Adam who is Christ is now living in the believer.

A Christian, according to Paul , is a person who has overcome problems between Jews and Gentiles, between male and female, and between a slave and a free man. In fact , a Christian is a person who is struggling with more and less successful to achieve this idealized social order. Another problem with most Christians of the first

47

century was their disappointment of not seeing the kingdom of God is fully accomplished. They wanted to see Christ coming back on earth.

2 . THE CONCEPT OF DEATH AND RESURRECTION

Paul believes that those who accept Jesus as their Savior and Lord suffered the same acts Jesus went through, these are death and resurrection. When Paul wrote the Letter to the Romans, he said : " Therefore, brothers and sisters, we have an obligation—but it is not to the flesh, to live according to it. For if you live according to the flesh, you will die; but if by the Spirit you put to death the misdeeds of the body, you will live."(Rom 8:12-13). This is said about those who have died with Christ and who are now living in him, those who are born in the Spirit of Christ, the Spirit of God or the Holy Spirit.

3 . CONSEQUENCES OF THE CHRISTIAN'S DEATH

There are privileges for the Christian's dead as well as his rise with Christ. These privileges are the true conditions of every believer . This new life separates the old man who has received the death sentence pronounced against him fully conviction and the new one who lives in Christ. In this context, the flesh is neither recognized, excused nor accepted. The old nature is inherently bad for the Christian . It must be eliminated and be replaced with a new nature and be possessed by Christ. From this level, the Christian receives the blessings individually and collectively as an Assembly of the

48

Saints. The Christian lives in intimacy with God , he lives in God the Father's grace , God the Father , it is the body of Christ.

Listen to what Paul says in Ephesians " predestined us in love to be his adopted children through Jesus Christ, according to the good pleasure of his will (Ephesians 1:5). Christian lives in the peace of God which passes all comprehension (Phil.4 : 7) , he lives in a huge divine grace (Ephesians 2: 10; 1 Cor 3: 9.).
Theses blessings and privileges are given to him by God himself . They allow him to enjoy communion with God under two conditions: be faithful and obedient to God.

4 . OPPOSITION TO THE BODY AND THE MIND

The Christian is someone who lives in war all his life on this earth. This war is between the one he is and the person he has become. That is because he is still a human being born of a woman who still has feelings, human desires , the heart and lives in an environment which is as corrupted and ruled by Satan and his agents.   At the same time this is the person who has given herself body and soul to the Lord ; a person who is the temple of the Holy Spirit (1 Cor 6.12-20) and he is a member of the body of Christ (1 Cor 12, 27) son or daughter of God. This person is now called to do the will of God always, and he is the one who knows that the wages of sin is death.

The opposition between the body and the Spirit is what characterizes the life of a Christian. His calling it to create new behaviors through the Spirit. Paul sees both the manifestation of that freedom for which Christ "We has released " (Gal 5:1) He writes: . .

49

" You were called to freedom , brethren , only do not use your freedom as an opportunity for the flesh, but through love be servants of one other for all the law is fulfilled in one word : Thou shalt love thy neighbor as thyself " (Gal. 5:13-14) . As we have already pointed out, the opposition body / mind , life according to the flesh / life according to the Spirit permeates deeply throughout the Pauline doctrine of justification. With exceptional strength of conviction, the Apostle of the Gentiles proclaims that justification is accomplished in Christ and through Christ . Man gets justification by " faith working through love" (Gal 5:6) , and not only through the observation of the individual requirements of law of the Old Testament (especially those of the circumcision) . The Justification therefore, is in " the Spirit " (God) and not in " the flesh. " Paul exhorts the recipients of his letter to free themselves from carnal mistaken notion of justification, to follow the true, which is spiritual. In this sense, he urges them to consider themselves free from the law , and not to be free from the freedom for which Christ " freed us . " In this way, following the thought of the Apostle , we should consider and live by a especial evangelical purity which is the purity of heart , according to the measure of that freedom for which Christ " freed us . "

5 . A CHRISTIAN DOES NOT LIVE IN SIN

When Paul speaks of the need to put to death the deeds of the body with the help of the Spirit, he expresses precisely what Christ said in the Sermon on the Mount , urging the man to control his desires, and not satisfy the desires of the flesh. This control is what Paul refers to " put to death the deeds of the body with the help of the Spirit." It is an essential condition of living in the Spirit. Living according to the flesh has death as its fruit.

Thus, the term "dead" means not only physical death but also the death of sin, moral theology speaks about "mortal" . In the letters to the Romans and the Galatians , the apostle continually widens the horizon of "de death o sin". After enumerating the multiform works of the flesh , he says that "those who practice such things will not inherit the kingdom of God " (Gal 5:21) . Moreover, he wrote with a similar firmness : " Make sure , that no fornicator or unclean idolater has any inheritance in the kingdom of God"   (Ephesians 5:5).

6 . A CHRISTIAN IS ASSOCIATED WITH CHRIST .

According to Paul , once the person believes in Jesus, that means he has given his life to him, he dies and rises with him. So right now , although he is still living on this earth and is the same person, physically and externally , he has become a new creation, and now he lives in Christ and for him. He has become closely united with Christ by the power of the Holy Spirit who dwells in him. He has also become the body of Christ as a member of his Church. This person so united to Christ becomes a child of God .

In Ephesians , Paul develops the privileges of the child of God from his death in the flesh and his union with Christ. In Colossians , Paul develops the foundation of his teaching that a Christian who has died and was raised with Christ, Christ lives and becomes manifested in his life from that time in the way he will be manifested with Christ in his glory .

The new nature of the Christian is seen in Colossians; and Christ united with the new man in the Spirit is taught in Ephesians. This is the way Christians become "members of the body of Christ.

7. A CHRISTIAN SEEN THROUGH CHRIST

In Ephesians the Christian is seen in Christ , not Christ in the Christian . We are thus led to consider the privileges of the Christian and of the Assembly of saints and the fullness of Christ in them. We find more here a contrast between the new position that we were in the world and the new one we are now in Christ. The development of the life of Christ in the Christian is widely treated in the Epistle to the Colossians, which considers Christ in the life of the Christians. Contrary to the Ephesians , a Christian is found in Christ with God the Father, who is seated in heavenly places (Col.3 : 2). Paul's testimony here, proves that Christ is in him, he becomes active and responsible in his daily life because of Christ in him.

8 . THE HOLY SPIRIT IN THE CHRISTIAN

When the Holy Spirit comes to dwell in our heart , he produces in us a new way of life because we live and are led by the Spirit. The life of the believer becomes a different one.(Galatians 5:19-21-22)

There is a clear contrast between the works of the flesh and the fruit of the spirit. Christian , because of the Holy Spirit who dwells in him

, should produce the fruits of the Spirit.

The Holy Spirit produces in the Christian new thoughts : those of God, new feelings : those of Christ , new desires his own desires . new affections : that God loves.

Those who live according to the flesh love the things of the flesh, but those who live according to the Spirit, the things of the spirit . They are affectionate by of the this of God, love of God, peace and so forth. If the Spirit of God , the spirit of Christ dwells in us , we no longer live according to the flesh but according to the Spirit. (Romans 8:9) . The Holy Spirit who dwells in us, drives us toward holiness, because He is holy.

9 . ATTRIBUTES OF GOD

Talking about God's attributes is dealing with his personality traits which fall into two broad categories: incommunicable attributes: what belong to God alone, from his divinity , and communicable attributes: that God reveals to us and communicates to a certain extent, himself to his children.

Some incommunicable attributes are: **God is infinite** , that is to say, he is everywhere; nothing can escape (1 Kings 8.27 ; Acts 17.24-28) . In this context, one also speaks of God's immensity . This means that the Creator is no subject to space limitations.

God is one. It is a single indivisible by his essence. We find this statement in the confession of traditional faith of Israel, the Shema . " Hear, O Israel ! The LORD our God is one Lord "(Deuteronomy 6:4) . The New Testament idea of Trinity does not contradict this assertion of the unity of God .

God is sovereign. He has all power in heaven and on earth. He is clothed with absolute authority over all creation. His sovereignty , God also maintains all things, and everything is subordinate (Genesis 14:19 , Deuteronomy 10.14

God has full knowledge of everything. He has absolute knowledge of everything that has existed, exists and will exist , knowledge of God is infinite knowledge (omniscience) . Unlike human beings, who can only observe external things and have limited knowledge , God sees and penetrates to the deepest human thoughts (Heb.4:13).

10. SOME COMMUNICABLE ATTRIBUTES

God is truth . The Bible includes many ideas in this word as truth , loyalty , for example. This means that the Scriptures have a perfectly trustworthy God is the absolute source of all truth in all areas of life.

God is merciful . Compassion or mercy, is related to another attribute called goodness. We can define the compassion of God as God's goodness manifested toward people who are in distress, without the merits thereof may be put forward. It must be stressed that God's compassion is always exercised in harmony with his justice considers the sin merits of Jesus Christ.

God is free. Freedom means that God totally independent of his creatures and his creation . God has no obligation to the one and the other , but in His grace and in His sovereignty , yet he chooses to do things freely. This means that he owes us nothing.

God is patient. This is yet another aspect of the goodness of God.

Because of his patience, God supports those who oppose him .
Because of his patience, he pushes at the later day the judgment
which is deserved to man who refused to repent (Ro. 2.4 , 9.22) .
God is holy in himself . (2 Timothy 4: 8)
God is just . This is closely related to his holiness. This is holiness
in action.

God acts righteously . His righteousness is the standard of conduct .
(1 Thessalonians 5: 24) **God is faithful** . We fully believe in his
words, which is always fulfilled .

God is love. Because of this, God wants a personal relationship with
us . This is why he wants the good of man .
God is good. It is the source of all that is good. Complimentary sake
of God is revealed in the care he deploys for the good of His
creatures. For man is in communication with God the Holy Spirit to
guide it faithful and obedient to God.

When we walk with God, when we walk in the Spirit without
grieve the Spirit keeps us in communion, in the enjoyment of God,
positive source of joy, a joy forever. This is a position in which God
holds us in developing its advice, his glory , his goodness , and grace
in the person of Jesus, the Christ , the Son of his love. This is the
normal condition of the Christian. This was , in fact, the case of
Ephesians .

CHAPTER IV

A CHRISTIAN ACCORDING
TO PAUL

1. THE NEW MAN IN AN OLD BODY

As we have said before, Paul believes that when we speak about a
Christian we speak about someone lives, not according to the life he
knew when he was born, but the one who lives according to the
Spirit and Christ because of his new birth. His old man is dead and
he is a new creation in Christ.   The following verses confirm Paul's
position:

"Knowing that our old man was crucified with him." (Rom. 6:6) .

"Those who are Christ's have crucified the flesh." (Gal. 5: 34).

"If by the Spirit you mortify the deeds of the body , ye shall live ."

Paul advises Christians to death the earthly man (Col. 8:5). So
according to him , the man , the person who bears the name of
Christian is the heavenly man . (Rom. 7: 18).

Paul speaks of two Adams to mean both creation "That is why it
is written, The first man Adam became a living soul .That we are

descendants of Adam and Eve we inherited this mortal , sinful nature

Paul believes that a person who accepts Jesus as his Savior and Lord suffered the same things Jesus suffered in his death and resurrection. When Paul writes in the Letter to the Romans: " Therefore, brethren , we are debtors, not to the flesh, to live according to the flesh , for if you live according to the flesh you will die , but if by the Spirit you put mortify the deeds of the body, ye shall live "(Rom 8:12-13) it is for those who have died with Christ and who are now living in him. He aimed at those who are born in the Spirit of Christ, the Spirit of God or the Holy Spirit.

2 . HE IS A HOLY GOD IS COME SAINT

A new person, a believer is manifested in his new daily life in Christ. That person has a model, Jesus Christ himself. That is why Paul says," Therefore be the imitators of God, as beloved children (Eph.5 :1 -2)

In the first Adam, what we have become is sinners. In Jesus, what the believers have become is holy, »But now you must be holy in everything you do, just as God who chose you is holy. For the Scriptures say, "You must be holy because I am holy." (1 Pet 1.15-16.)

The scriptures use several expressions to express the object, and the purpose of our calling. Paul says it well in this first letter to Thessalonians, " For God called us not for uncleanness, but in sanctification. (I Thess. 4 :7) That idea of sanctification is what God does in the life of those who have untrusted their lives to him, { And the very God of peace sanctify you wholly; and I pray God your whole spirit and soul and body be preserved blameless unto the coming of our Lord Jesus Christ (I Thessal. 5:23) ."

In 2 Timothy I, 9, Paul calls this calling from God a "holy calling." - " It is He who has sent us a holy calling ." "In him , God chose us to be holy and blameless ."   (2 Thes.2 :13) .

A misunderstanding of the call and the place of a person who is born again in Christ should be as clear to the callee as pure dringing water inside a glass . Because of who the Ephesians have become as God elected to be holy, Paul prayed for them to be " I keep asking that the God of our Lord Jesus Christ, the glorious Father, may give you the Spirit of wisdom and revelation, so that you may know him better. " (Eph. 1:17). This is the hope to which they were called ."

The Christians' call is for holiness, "Since He who called you is holy , you also be holy ." It is as if God were saying, " Holiness is my nature and my glory; without it you can not, in any way be close or see me.

God's holiness contaminates our daily life and human relationsihps.

God does not only said, "I am holy ," but " I am the Lord who sanctifies you." God invites us to remember that his holiness is the one which makes us holy. He calls us to follow the ways and the teachings of the Spirit. He invites us to give ourselves to him so he can instill in us the will to become like our Lord Jesus Christ.

A Christian is a sinner is born again. His outward man is the same as that of its interior is totally addicted to the Spirit because he is a new creation . For who hath known the mind of the Lord to instruct ? We can see that which is born of the Spirit carries him two personalities , physical or animal personality and spiritual personality. Because he is born of the Spirit , born in Christ, he is walking in the Spirit and not after the flesh

4 . HE DIES IN SIN AND ALIVE IN CHRIST

This passage from the Letter to the Romans 6 :11 -23 describes very well the concept of death to sin and alive in Christ . "Do not yield your members to sin as instruments of unrighteousness , but give yourselves to God as being alive from the dead you were, and offer God your members as instruments of righteousness . For sin shall not have dominion over you: for you are not under law, but under grace . "

The man born again , man freed , the man born of the Holy Spirit , that man in Christ is dead to sin . The term " dead to sin " according to Paul , is not figurative, but in reality.
Be dead to sin means being incapable of sinning . James writes things very clear on the subject of temptation and sin. " Nobody

should say , when tempted : It is God who tempts me . For God can not be tempted by evil, and he himself tempts no one. But each one is tempted when he is lured and enticed by his own lust . Then when lust hath conceived, it bringeth forth sin: and sin when it is finished, bringeth forth death. (James 1 , 13-15).

Since it is human and still bears the physical caricature like Jesus , and he may be tempted to follow the path of Jesus to triumph over temptation and glorify God by doing so.

Our faith is then tested , resulting in the salvation of our soul. The gospel message is that even though it is tempting , it is not obliged to sin - was the knowledge that the wages of sin is death, but those who are victorious will have eternal life ! (Romans 6: 23)

5 . SUFFERING IN CONTROL .

1 Peter 4 says "Therefore , since Christ suffered in the flesh, arm yourselves also with the same mind" . If you read the whole chapter of I Peter 4 , it would be understood that we, Christians of the 21st century , have a poor understanding of what it means to be a Christian . Pierre advises Christians to arm themselves with the thought of suffering. Listen to how we pray ! We spend the majority of our time in prayer asking God to take away from us any suffering, all financial headaches financial, all sicknesses . No Christian today prays for patience, for understanding, for perseverance that they become strong in persecution, in the faith because of social events or else.

Jesus had a lot of enemies in this world. He said that all those who bear his name will be persecuted . He reminds us of what is coming when he says, "You will be hated by all because of my name" (Luke 21 : 17). Paul also says this to the believers in 2 Timothy 3.12 "All that will live godly in Christ Jesus shall suffer persecution ."

Unfortunately , the Christian still has the heart and carnal desires . As long as he is alive, he will remain a member of the human society. His call to live under the guidance of the Spirit makes him a soldier fighting against himself, his fellow men and Satan. He must every hour, every day resist and fight to say "no"; refuse shortcuts, to go with the current, but remain pure refusing the easy way out, the let it go, compromise, lies, etc. .

We are mistaken to believe that the Christian life is like someone said , **"The Christian life is not a bed of roses "** . We shall neveer forget that the enemy of our Master is still alive, and he is also our enemy. As he attacked Christ , it's our turn to be attacked .

The following passages trace the path of the life of new men in Christ during our lives on earth. (a) First, we must continually walk in the light (1 John 1:7) " But if we walk in the light as he himself is in the light, we have fellowship one with another , and the blood of Jesus his Son cleanses us from all sin. (b) We must always acknowledge our sin and confess them immediately (I John 1 :8 -10) " If we say we have no sin , we deceive ourselves, and the truth is not in us.

If we confess our sins, he is faithful and just to forgive us and to cleanse us from all unrighteousness.

If we say we have not sinned , we make him a liar , and his word is not in us . "

(c) We must continually flee from sin (I John 2:1-2) My little children, these things write I unto you , that ye sin not. And if anyone sins , we have an advocate with the Father, Jesus Christ the righteous .

And he is the propitiation for our sins: and not for ours only but also for the world.

By confession and repentance , the blood of Jesus comes again purify our hearts and allows us to think of things from above.

These verses in Colossians lay the foundation on which the inner man becomes addicted to the Spirit and Christ builds his house (Colossians 3:1-3) " If you then be risen with Christ, seek the things above where Christ is seated at the right hand of God .

Set your affection on things above , not on things on the earth. For you died , and your life is hidden with Christ in God. "

Christian remembers that nothing can separate him from the love of God in Christ. It is for this reason that Paul , though prison, could address this exhortation to the Philippians , " Rejoice in the Lord always , again I say . Let your gentleness be known to all men. The Lord is near . Do not worry about anything , but in everything bring your requests before God, by prayer and supplication with thanksgiving . And the peace of God which surpasses all understanding , will guard your hearts and your minds in Christ Jesus . For the rest , brethren, whatsoever things are true, whatever those who are honest, all those who are righteous , all those who are pure, all those lovely, whatever those are reputable , and where there any virtue , and worthy of praise, that all these things occupy your thoughts. You have also learned and received and heard from me , and you have seen me. Let them , and the God of peace will be with you all the circumstances of life. "(Philippians 4 :4 -9).

6 . HE IS IN THE WORLD BUT NOT FROM THE WORLD

We have covered the idea of a Christian descending from the first man, Adam. He was born and lived in sin. In the Old Testament , although the Israelites had the Law of Moses, they could not keep . Gentiles with an informed conscience although having the law of God in nature, also refused to acknowledge God. It is for this reason that both groups of people are without excuse . (Rom 1: 20). Therefore all have sin and come short of the glory of God. (Rom.3 : 23).

When a person becomes a Christian , he leaves this world to become a child of God. Before being a Christian, he was a slave to sin , but when he becomes to Christ, he becomes a slave to Jesus. " But thanks be to God that, though you used to be slaves to sin, you have come to obey from your heart the pattern of teaching that has now claimed your allegiance. You have been set free from sin and have become slaves to righteousness » (Rom.6 :17 -18).The Christian is in the midst of the world and he must accept it, or else he must leave the world to live according to the Spirit . (1 Cor. 5:9 : 13)

Christians are called to live in the world without being of the world , we must express our difference as children of God , born again.

"Do not strain out just in the mold of everyone Do not conform your life to the principles governing this century . Did not copy patterns and habits of the day. Let yourself rather completely transformed by the renewing of your mind . . Adopt a different inner attitude . Give your thoughts a new direction in order to discern what God wants from you . so you will be able to recognize what is right in his eyes, what he likes and which leads you to real maturity . " (Romans 12:2).

(1 Peter 4:3) That's enough, in fact, have in the past time doing the desire of the Gentiles, when we walked in lasciviousness , lusts , drunkenness, surfeiting , and drunkenness, and idolatry criminal .

Here's what Jesus said to those who followed his disciples , " You are the light of the world ... A lamp can not remain hidden ... You are the salt of the earth. The salt must retain its flavor ... You are my witnesses . A witness must not be silent ...
He even continued to say , "Let your light so shine before men, that they may see your good works , and glorify your Father which is in heaven.

Still in the Beatitudes , " (Matthew 5:13) You are the salt of the earth. But if the salt have lost his savor, wherewith shall it do you ? It serves only to be thrown out and trampled by men.

He made this recommendation to the apostles before his ascension (Acts 1:8) " But you shall receive power when the Holy Spirit comes on you, and you will be my witnesses in Jerusalem, throughout Judea , in Samaria, and to the ends of the earth.
Paul says that Christians must be blameless and harmless , children

of God without fault in a crooked and perverse generation, among whom they shine as lights in the world, holding fast the word of life. (Philippians 2:15)

Here is what Peter says about Christians who live like the world, " For if after they have escaped the defilements of the world by knowing our Lord and Savior Jesus Christ , they are again entangled therein, and overcome , the latter end is worse than the first (2 Peter 2:20) Jacques 1: 27 says that " pure religion and undefiled before God and the Father is this, to visit the fatherless and widows in their affliction, and to keep himself unspotted the world. "

Titus speaks of denying ungodliness and worldly lusts , and living soberly, righteously , and godly in the present age .(Titus 2.12).

Paul speaks of the wisdom of the world which is foolishness to God. (1 Cor. 1:20-21)

Paul asks that Christians stay away from the world and its vanities , its adulterated pleasures , its false joys, impure distractions , his wealth, his property, his thirst power, pride of life. (I Tim. 6 :7 -16)

While John makes this recommendation to Christians, "Love not the world, neither the things that are in the world . If anyone loves the world, the love of the Father is not in him for all that is in the world , the lust of the flesh, the lust of the eyes , and the pride of life, is not the Father, but is of the world. And the world passeth away, and the lust thereof: but he that doeth the will of God abides forever . " (I John 2 :15 -17)

Living under the prince of the power of the world , is to live in rebellion against God, " ... in which you once walked according to the course of this world, according to the prince of the power of the air, the spirit that now worketh in the son of disobedience (Ephesians 2.2)

Here is what every Christian should recite as a creed coming from Galatians 6.14 " For me, far be it from me to glorify me anything but the cross of our Lord Jesus Christ , by whom the world is crucified for me, as I am for the world! "

7 . IT IS NOT THE WORLD

The world is attractive , its subtle pleasures. The world promises much but gives very little. But if we fall in love with the world, our love for God is cool. We have already said that it is impossible to love two things without reserve. Jesus said the same thing in Matthew 6:24 - "No man can serve two masters : for either he will hate the one and love the other , or he will hold to the one , and despise the other . . Ye can not serve God and mammon . "

Jacques is even clearer : "Do not you know that friendship with the world is enmity against God whosoever therefore will be a friend of the world makes himself an enemy of God? ". Love for God and love for the world are incompatible.

Christians are the salt of the earth, which means that it must strive to make the pleasant world by his exemplary conduct in the midst of unbelievers. As the light of the world , he must enlighten the Gentiles by his remarkable fidelity to the Word of God.

I Mat. 5 :13 -16.) This is what Jesus said.

But the devil does not want that . All his effort is focused on one goal: to losen the taste of salt and make Christians less effective in their witnessing to the world. As he acting in the dark, he mobilized all his cunnings means to extinguish any light around him . The devil told a whopper : ' the end justifies the means". This leads many to get enriched through theft, lies, corruption , even murder ...In so doing , they become enemies of God. (Isaiah 5 :8 -18)

Contrary to that, he Lord teaches us justice as himself is just in all his ways . He expects that Christians be full of love and have a pure heart . (1 Thessalonians 4: 7), that they live in holiness , that their hearts mouths be pure, they be humble and seek to glorify the Lord always (Philippians 2 :3 -4) God calls Christians to be honest vis- à-vis others, even in small things . (1 Thessalonians 4: 5) and love God more than the things of this world in order not to lose their souls in hell (Galatians 6 :7 -8)

The Christian must consider themselves foreigners here and citizen of the kingdom of heaven (1 Peter 1: 11) Christians are not supposed to be conformed to this world or share same interests with the world; they are from a different world, and they are awaiting for the return of their Savior and Redeemer, Lord Jesus Christ. (Philippians 3:20

8 . HE LIVES IN THE SPIRIT

Someone said that " the Holy Spirit has a great ambition: to make every Christian a masterpiece of art. As a painter , he painted on the tablet of their lives the icon of Jesus Christ throughout the seasons of our lives ".

The Holy Spirit wants create in each Christians the image of Christ. Therefore, it is importance to let him take over, to be led by the Spirit, to enter the School of Christ. As a teacher, he takes us by the hand so that we learn how to live Christ's life .

A Christian who lives in and is inhabited by Christ abandons himself to the Spirit, to be shaped, form and be transformed in Christ by the Spirit; this is what is called the Life in the Spirit or spiritual life. The spiritual life is not confined to one area or at a certain section of our lives. The spiritual life is everything that makes human life. The Christian's cross fertilizes, quickenes ,and raises the high winds of the Spirit so nothing which is human be part of the life of a true believer.

To avoid false starts in the spiritual life , we must remember the four basic criteria. (1) allow Christ and his Spirit live in the Christians and let themselves be soaked by the Spirit and Christ. The starting point for this criterion is their death and resurrection with Christ. This is the heart of the spiritual life. (2) open to the Word of God in its two forms : written and preached Word and the Word received in the form of sacraments. Any devaluation of the sacraments , of not taking them seriously or false belief would be considered error. (3) The inclusion of our sinful human reality or the humble recognition of the need to be saved by an Other, that is by the Savior . Awareness of the two states and the need to abandon the first leads to live in the Spirit. (4) They must take into account the ecclesial element. It is important to belong to a Church - this church whose cornerstone is CHRIST himself - that church made up of saints and sinners who love their Savior.

Christians who walk according to the Spirit must always listen and remain reconciled to two masters : their conscience and God who is just, right , holy, omnipresent, omniscient and alive. Be reconciled both in their judgments , decisions , actions, and ways . In no way they should irritate the Holy Spirit who dwell in them. (Eph.6 : 4).

9 . IT IS JUSTIFIED IN CHRIST

Thia citation from Peter says it well, " Knowing that it is not by perishable things such as silver or gold that you were redeemed from the empty way of life you inherited from your fathers, but with the precious blood of Christ, as of a lamb without blemish and without spot " (I Peter 1 :18 -19)

Every born-again Christian was actually bought at a very expensive price , namely the " precious blood of Christ." The high price of the precious blood of Christ was absolutely necessary to atone for our sins ! The debt of sin could be paid only by " the precious blood of Christ ," the result of that pris is the justification of the sinner. Our Holy God almighty , could have no fellowship with the sinner before

that payement made. Holiness and purity of God on the one hand ,
the sin and uncleanness of man on the other excluded each other just
as fire does with water. At the same time , the Triune God was
willing to sacrifice the immortal God who became man in Jesus
Christ to shed His blood and die on the cross at Golgotha . That is
why this unique sacrifice of the Son of God has an eternal value and
total efficiency. This shows us how important we are to God. His
love for us is manifested in the sacrifice of His only Son whose
blood was shed on the cross. This unfathomable love of the Lord ,
Paul describes it saying, " But God demonstrates His own love
toward us, in that while we were yet sinners, Christ died for us " (
Romans 5: 8) This death Jesus has the following implications :

1. We have the forgiveness of our sins because of the blood " ...
almost all things are by the law, we are cleansed by the blood of
Christ. Without shedding of blood there is no possibility forgiveness
. " (Hebrews 9: 22)

2. We have redemptions because of this blood, Paul writes, " In him
we have redemption through his blood, the forgiveness of sins,
according to the riches of his grace. "
(Ephesians 1: 7)

3. We receive the purification by the same blood of Christ. John says
, "... but if we walk in the light as he himself is in the light, we have \
fellowship one with another , and the blood of Jesus his Son cleanses

70

us from all sin. " (1 John 1 : 7)

Christian guilt is washed , saved and redeemed by the blood of Jesus. It may have purified themselves before God. This is the only way that communion with the God of holiness is possible!

4. We are justified by that blood of Christ. Paul says this in Romans 5: 9 " Much more then, being now that we are justified by his blood, shall we be saved by him from the wrath . "

5. We have and live in peace with God through the blood : The Epistle to the Colossians says, "For God has willed that all his fullness dwell in him, he wanted by him (Jesus Christ) to reconcile all things to himself , whether things on earth or things in heaven , making peace by him, by the blood of his cross. " (Col. 1: 19-20)

6. Our sanctification is done every day because of this blood : Paul says in Hebrews "This is why Jesus also might sanctify the people through his own blood, suffered outside the gate . " (Heb. 13: 12)

7. We now have access to the Father because of the blood : " Therefore, brothers , since we have , by the blood of Jesus, a free entry into the sanctuary. " (Hebrews 10: 19)

As members of The Church of Jesus Christ, we Christians have become the temple in which the Holy Spirit dwells.

(1 Cor. 3 /16 - 17).

8. Jesus Christ won our eternal redemption. His sacrifice is valid forever. He Now represents our family before the heavenly Father: " ... he entered once for all into the holy place ... with his own blood, having obtained eternal redemption ... now to appear for us before the face of God. " (Heb. : 9: 12-24)

9. Another very important implication for the believers is : " You , on the contrary , you are a chosen race, a royal priesthood, a holy nation , a peculiar people , that ye should shew forth the praises of him who called you out of darkness into his marvelous light , you who once were not a people, but are now the people of God: which had not obtained mercy, but now have obtained mercy . " (1 Peter 2: 9-10)

10. We glorified God because of the blood of Christ on the cross. And those he intended , he also called; those he has called, he also justified , and those whom he has declared righteous , he also led them to glory. "(Romans 8:30)

10 . HE IS LIVING WAITING OF THE LORD

Two important events will take place at the same time according to two passages found in I Corinthians 15 and I Thessalonians 4 namely the return of Jesus Christ and the advent of resurrection. These two are very important for the Church of Jesus Christ in general and for each believer in particular. They depend one on the other. Here is what Paul says in first Thessalonians chapter 4 and verse 13: " We do not want not that you be ignorant towards those sleeping (dead) so that you do not grieve as do the others who have no hope. for if we believe that Jesus died and that ' He is risen , as well as with him , God will bring those who have fallen asleep in Jesus, as we say unto you by the word of God : "We are alive and remain unto the coming of the Lord shall not precede not those who have fallen asleep . For the Lord himself, with a cry of command, with the voice of the archangel and with the trumpet of God shall descend from heaven and the dead in Christ shall rise first: then we which are alive and remain, shall be caught up together with them in the clouds to meet the Lord in the air. And so shall we ever be with the Lord. Wherefore comfort one another with these words . "

Jesus Christ returns at the end of the world to make those who belong to Him , those who have given to him and took his Words seriously. Those who did not believe in him will be judged and condemned for eternity.

The return of Jesus Christ will be the starting of unprecedented global crisis .

First what evidence do we have the return of Jesus Christ?

When the Lord knew his approaching death, that He would offer his great sacrifice, shed his blood for the sins of all who believe in him, knowing also that his disciples would remain sad, lonely and orphans, he told them this word in the Gospel of (John 14:1)

" Let not your heart be troubled not : believe in God, believe also in me in my Father's house , there are many mansions If it were otherwise I would . . would have said. and if I go and prepare a place for you I , I will come back and take you to myself that where I am you , you may be also. " Therefore, Jesus Christ returns to fulfill his promise .

The return of Jesus Christ is one of the most important biblical teachings .

The New Testament tells us about 9 times about the new birth , he speaks of baptism 20 times , 70 times concerning repentance and more than 300 times concerning the return of Jesus Christ.

The Old Testament and New Testament are filled with more prophecies concerning the second coming of Jesus Christ. And since the former were fulfilled , we guarantee that the other will be fulfilled too.

I can not guarantee that I will see my bed tonight , I can not guarantee I kiss my family tomorrow morning or I greet the new year, but if there is one thing I can guarantee and I am absolutely certain is that Jesus Christ returns .

The second question we ask ourselves is this : When the Lord will he return ?

It is impossible to fix the date of his return ! When the disciples, a little time before his ascension, asked him this question: " Is it these days you restoring the kingdom to Israel the Lord told them :" This is not for you know the times or seasons that the Father has reserved his own authority " But despite these clear words of the Lord , some have tried to find the date of his return.

Thus, a Christian sect , for scientific calculations , found that Christ would return somewhere in the 1860s. They were so sure ! Together, they waited ... in vain. They called it their first disappointment. They then again better than the first calculations . And they called their second disappointment.

As they had more in ideas, they even set a third a little more discreet than the first two dates , it was their third disappointment ! So do not expect someone to give you the date of the return of Jesus Christ. If I gave dates, I find myself in the embarrassing situation of Jehovah's Witnesses who , after the erroneous 1914 , prophesied without possibility of error this time , the new date was in 1975.

CHAPTER V

CHRISTIAN AND CHURCH ENEMIES.

1 . CHRISTIAN HIS OWN ENEMY

According to the Bible , the Christian is one who is baptized into the death and resurrection of Christ. He died and was resurrected with Christ. He was baptized in his own death (Rom. 6 :3 -11). He also raised in his new nature with Christ.Paul says this in addressing to the new man in Christ, "Since, then, you have been raised with Christ, set your hearts on things above, where Christ is, seated at the right hand of God. Set your minds on things above, not on earthly things. For you died, and your life is now hidden with Christ in God. When Christ, who is your life, appears, then you also will appear with him in glory" (Colossians 3:1-4).

The man is now a man born again, a new creation. As was Jesus who lived on this 40 days after his resurrection was a new Jesus, the Christian who died in his baptism and raised with Christ does no longer live in the flesh but in the Spirit . What I mean is that he still bears the physical and human body but is no longer under his

76

domination.

There is a concept that ANY true Christian must understand. Once born in Christ by faith in Christ's death on the cross, the Christian becomes a saint. It is "supposed" to sin no more; he is sanctified and has already chosen who he is, who is his master, whom he will serve for the remaining of his life on this earth; he becomes a slave of Jesus and not of Satan. James says everything that would try to deviate him from that road is not a temptation but a " test ." It is to see at what level is his faith, his devotion and love to his Master , the level of its relations with God, his appreciation of what God has already done for him, his level of maturity in faith, of his sanctification , of regeneration , of hope in God, of his commitment and of his knowledge of the Scriptures and status as Christian. That is why James 1 :2 -4 says, "Brothers , look like the subject of a perfect joy the various temptations that come to you , knowing that the testing of your faith produces patience. But let patience have its perfect work , that ye may be perfect and complete, lacking in nothing " When a Christian fails a test, he is telling God that he doesn't have enough faith. When he wins he proves to God and to himself that he has a higher level of faith and commitment to God.

The first enemy of the Christian is himself when he disappoints himself and God who already elevates him in the rank of a saint in his eyes.

Every Christian must therefore undertake and win an eternal war in himself. When I say this, I hear Paul saying , " For we know that the law is spiritual, but I am of the flesh, sold under sin. [15] For I do not understand my own actions. For I do not do what I want, but I do the very thing I hate. [16] Now if I do what I do not want, I agree with the law, that it is good. [17] So now it is no longer I who do it, but sin that dwells within me. [18] For I know that nothing good dwells in me, that is, in my flesh. For I have the desire to do what is right, but not the ability to carry it out " (Romans 7:14-18).

Even Paul continues by saying " Now if I do what I do not want to do, it is no longer I who do it, but it is sin living in me that does it. So I find this law at work: Although I want to do good, evil is right there with me. For in my inner being I delight in God's law; but I see another law at work in me, waging war against the law of my mind and making me a prisoner of the law of sin at work within me. What a wretched man I am! Who will rescue me from this body that is subject to death?" (Romans 7 :20- 24).
This is where all Christians this is the cry of all Christians this is the fight that should be notified every Christian. To overcome , we must abandon the Lord and the Holy Spirit.

Here's what Paul said after finding his inability to cope with this situation, and especially the change, he says, " The grace of God through Jesus Christ our Lord. So I myself am subject to the spirit of God's law , but by the flesh the law of sin". (Ro. 7: 25)

Being aware of who we are we will always rest on the grace and power of God who loves us with an everlasting love . Paul affirms with a hopeful nothing and nothing can separate us from the love of God in Jesus Christ tone. " What shall we say in response to these things? If God is for us, who can be against us ? He who did not spare his own Son, but delivered him up for us all, how will he not also give us all things with him? Who acknowledge God's elect ? It is God who justifies ! Who condemns? Christ died , yea rather, that is risen again, who is at the right hand of God and is also interceding for us! Who shall separate us from the love of Christ? Shall tribulation , or distress , or persecution , or famine , or nakedness , or peril , or sword ? as it is written : It is for your sake we are being killed all day long , we are accounted as sheep for the slaughter. But in all these things we are more than conquerors through him who loved us . For I am persuaded, that neither death, nor life , nor angels, nor principalities, nor things present nor things to come, nor powers, nor height, nor depth, nor any other creature can separate us from the love of God in Christ Jesus our Lord". (Rom.8 :31-39)

2 . THE WORLD IS HIS GREAT ENEMY

The second enemy is the world. The world can be the whole universe ; the symbol of the land inhabited by humans, or representing humanity and all human that God loves and wants to save. This world is hostile to the Word of God and rejects the Gospel of Jesus. This world with all its systems opposes Christ as well as his Church. It is against those who give it up for God . It is unfortunate that those holy men still live among their peers who are wicked and instruments of the devil . These become enemies of the new born now Christians. This world glorifies elements such as the lust of the flesh and eyes, the pride of life.

The world also symbolizes this century. "Do not be conformed to this world: but be transformed by the renewing of your mind , that you may prove what is the will of God, what is good and acceptable and perfect " (Romans 12:2) . Christians must fight this battle against the world and win, get to separate the precious (God's will) from the vile (will of the world) and walk by faith in Jesus. A true Christian must clearly identify the second enemy of his Christian life.

3 . SATAN IS HIS ENEMY

His third enemy is Satan. It is the strongest and the head of all Christians' enemies. He is a fallen angel. He is the leader of all the demons. He organizes and controls each physical area and spiritual of the world   (1 Timothy 4: 1 , Acts 16: 16). He attacks Christians in all areas of their lives. But Christ has given us the authority to trample on his plans for the weapons of our warfare are spiritual orders (2 Corinthians 10: 3 -6).

The Devil's strongholds in our lives that prevent us from moving forward , entering our blessings and graces that our Father have given to Christ and dead in us. But if Christians know how to use the weapons they have in order to fight not with flesh but by the power of God to reverse the plans and the agents of the devil, and will win our freedom in Christ always . (John 13: 17), because we stand on what the apostle John says, "You , dear children, are from God and have overcome them , because He who is in you is more greater than he who is in the world . " (1 John 4: 4).This is our hope.

4 . MORE THAN CONQUERORS

The words of Paul in Romans 8:37 affirm this hope, "we are more than conquerors through Christ who loves us". However, for this to happen , it is necessary that we know what are the ultimate predispositions we must we have toward God, the Devil and and everything around us. We also need to know our rights and privileges.

When the Lord God created the heavens and the earth , and formed human beings from the dust, he blessed them, saying, " Be fruitful , multiply, fill the earth and subdue it . Have dominion over the fish of the sea , over the birds of heaven and all the animals that swarm on the earth (Genesis 1:28) .

This statement from God makes us conquerors toward all circumstances. This is the ways God created us. We betrayed the Lord by sinning. We lost our authority and dominion over things; instead of dominating over them, we became their servants. Using what God has given to fulfill our needs and not our wants will be the first predisposition. The second disposition should be to put God first and ourselves second. God's needs and pleasures will be ours too.

Christians are here to joyfully give thanks to the Father who has qualified them to access the inheritance of the saints. He has delivered them from the authority of darkness to carry them into the kingdom of his beloved Son . (Colossians 1: 12,13)

The Lord God expects them to accept this condition, and that them can act like men more than conquerors . The devil knows that their real situation is well defined. On the other hand , he also knows that those who obey God will defeat him. Let us be in that number of conquerors. .

CHAPTER VI

WHAT IS THE CHURCH ?

OBJECTIVES OF THE CHURCH
OF THE 21ST CENTURY

Know what is happening today in the Old Christian world, with the loss of traditional Christianity identity and new phases of Christianity of the streets, the question that requires our response is this: What should Main Churches, namely traditional denominations included the Catholic Church, those Churches which have been the sources of the Good News of salvation in the world should do now?

1 . THE CHURCH IS IN CRISIS

These Main Traditional Christian Churches must first of all recognize they are going through a very deep and destructive identity crisis . This crisis has several causes. The first one is that many people who are their members claim to be Christians when they are not . It may not only be among the congregatants, but among the leaders, the clergy. These are not servants but are being served by these Churches and their institutions. Some are struggling to keep the comfortable, rules and physical organizations of the traditional past; but that doesn't hold any longer. Some are in search of an "authentic" experience. Others are looking for healing and wellness and nothing happens. In order to start the process, these main Churches must find the definition of true purpose of the Church of Jesus Christ on this earth. We are not talking about some individual church, but the Church of Jesus. Why did Jesus come to die on the cross? Are our individual church fulfilling that objective of the Son of God? As long as members and the leadership of each main denomination seem be and remain immune to what the Church is going through the crisis will continue, and the end of it will be the requiem.

2 . THE CHURCH IS DECEPTIVE

Main Traditional Christian Churches must identify areas in which they have disappointed God and their followers, those they have been called to bring the light of God. For some churches, it has been the burden imposed on the members who don't have any say it what is going on; for some others in may be the emptiness of spiritual food in what is going on; for some it may be the human side which has enter clerical ranks; some may say the way the church and the world have become similar, it would be like God has left his Church. The right answers to these issues are the only ways reabilitation will take place. Some of the answers will require surgical measures in order to rebuild the Church of Jesus Christ on earth.

3 . LET US FIND SOLUTIONS

Main Traditional Christian Churches must seek their place in the
society. Going to church on Sunday should not be the only goal of
those big buidings and well educated clergy who are ruining the
church. One, two or three hours a week should be out of the
question in order to reach that renewal of the Church. A good
sermon every 7 days will not be enough. Churches must find new
forms of services in order to have their place in the heart of the
people. These solutions must out of whatever churches are doing
right now . The proof is that all those who call themselves new
churches are not similar in their actions withing the society
compared to what all old denominations descendant from Luther's
Reformation do. If we continue doing what we do, our identity will
start agonizing, then die. Are you will to bury, as what is happening
now in Europe and msany places in ASmerica, sell your church in
order that the investors will transform those sacret places into
whatever?

4 . GOD NOT IN THE HEARTS

One of the solutions to end this crisis is to turn Christians' hearts to
God . The church must bring God is the center of the lives of the
believers. Believers don't see God's face, don't live God's fear,
don't hear God's voice and are not called to serve him. The
missionary Church of the past died long time ago .

85

When God is not fully integrate in the confession and the lives of the believers, when is is not in the making of their personal problems and community decisions , when he is not in their moral life and practice, when he is absent in the Church, we don't need more to know that it is dead.

5 .CHRIST NOT THE HEAD OF THE CHURCH

We must let Christ and his Spirit reign in his Church. When we silenced all other voices , if the Church of Jesus Christ is not submisive to his voice and will, when he is not recognize as the Head , when the new man, born of the Spirit and the blood of Christ is one who is not the body Christ, when the servant is served, the glory , the honor and the praise do not go to God but to the men , there is no way that the true identity of the Christ will be there. As long as the Church remains in the hands of the antichrists , the hypocrites, the thieves, and selfish men, people who are not regenerated, and those who are still in the flesh , the death of Main Traditional Christian Churches is certain.

Look at what is happening il all traditional Protestant Denominational Churches, including the Catholics starting from Europe, in countries such as Italy , Spain, Germany, France , England, Scotland, the Netherlands , Ireland, and now the United-States of America ! We do not know how much time is left for South America, Africa , the Philippines, and Japan. We who had lived for more than a quarter century among these civilized and Christian world can testify that it is not too late to start correcting the course

86

of our boat in developing countries. Whoever reads these pages knows that the sun of pure the Gospel of Jesus Christ which has been preached for the last 2,000 years it is more threatened today than ever. Our time the time to defend and redirect this message is now .

Jesus gave us the Good News to proclaim to the nations. The Great Commissions to make new disciples is strong today as it was at the first century. Once the church, any Christian Community, put in the back burner that commission, its reason to be is caught half. Seeking and saving souls is one of the permanent objectives of the Church of Jesus Christ on earth. A Spiritual church is a saving Christian Community.

7 . SOULS NOT CENTRE

The caring of human souls must be at the center of the work of the Church. The preparation for the return of our Lord Jesus Christ should be the center of Church activities and instructions. The strengthening of personal relationships between the believers and their God should concern the Church. A submissive attitude and service as a slave of his Master must prevail and lead the leaders of the Church in order to become good models for the congregations. When we read Paul's letters, he kept presenting himself to those he brought to Christ as a model they should follow. When the one who has been called to lead doesn't set himself as an imitator of Jesus Christ, from where Christ first and the rest will model themselves on those who have been modeled by Christ.

The identity, personality, the Great Commission, de souls of

87

the believers, the preparation of the return of Christ and the similar subjects should be goals and objectives of the Church. When the Church has her eyes fixed on Jesus, seeking his approval, this is an important sign that Jesus is the head, leaders are servants, souls are taken care of, and the glory and the honor belong to Jesus.

Spending time in prayer , confessing our sins , meditating on passages of Scripture which could inspired us, holding spiritual retreats, seeking personal and collective regeneration would do a lot of good to those who believe that we need new directions for the Church of Jesus Christ in this 21st century .

8 . THE CHURCH AS THE BODY OF CHRIST

The concept of the Church is totally from Paul; he is the one who created it . Until Paul came to the picture, the synagogue and the temple were where the rest of the apostles evolved. Paul developed around that concept the idea of the Body of Christ. Once the Gospel of the salvation is proclaimed, she draws all the saved into a community to which is given the name of the Church, from the Greek language " ecclesia " means " convocation ." In the Greek world there was a system to call the meeting of citizens to settle the affairs of the city and enact if necessary for the proper ordering of society laws.

Here is a description of the life of such communities according to their founder , Paul, " As a prisoners for the Lord, then, I urge you to live a life worthy of the calling you have received. Be completely humble and gentle; be patient, bearing with one another in love.

Make every effort to keep the unity of the Spirit through the bond of peace. There is one body and one Spirit, just as you were called to one hope when you were called; one Lord, one faith, one baptism; one God and Father of all, who is over all and through all and in all, But each of us was given grace according to the measure of Christ's gift". (Ephesians 4.1-7) .

When a Christian community takes the name of the Church, she is considered the people whom God has called . She obtains a legal status of a divine origin which makes her the people who belong to God, that Christ loves and for which he gave his life . This church is made up of holy people whose mission is to witness to the world the holiness of God and the mystery of salvation revealed in Jesus Christ : " Christ loved the Church and gave himself up for her, he sanctified purified and gave him his Word , she is beautiful, without stain or wrinkle or any such default and flawless". (Eph. 5:25-27)

The holiness of the Church comes from the holiness of her Founder , the thrice holy God . Therefore , it is the people who belong to God, the Body of Christ , Temple of the Spirit. It is united in love with the nature of the Father, the Son and the Spirit. The Church participates , despite the diversity of her members, in this divine unity resulted in the constant search for unity in the bond of peace , in the biblical sense meaning harmony , unanimity of hearts and well-being in its fullness.

The Church, as it appears in her visible form on earth, is not a static but a dynamic reality. The nature of the Church is to be holy , that is to remain entirely rooted in God . The Church which is spread over the earth is a community walking towards the realization of her vocation to holiness. It is not completed once a reality yet . Members of the Christian community are responsible for building up the body of Christ and bringing all to the unity in the faith and in the knowledge of the Son of God, the fullness of the Body of Christ. (John 17:3)) .

The pursuit of holiness is a common task to which all Christians must work together and this is the true Christian community ministry that performs as Paul says here , " Therefore, as God's chosen people, holy and dearly loved, clothe yourselves with compassion, kindness, humility, gentleness and patience". (Colossians 3:12) .

The Christian community must grow in Christ for the extension of God's Kingdom on the world. This community is the privileged place where the reality of salvation brought by Christ finds its full realization . Many exhortations by which Saint Paul asks Christians to live according to the calling they have received in this direction . (1 Cor 12: 8, 10) .

Christians are people who have a conscience, "They show that the requirements of the law are written on their hearts, their consciences also bearing witness, and their thoughts sometimes accusing them and at other times even defending them". (Romans 2 : 15) Consciousness is not a product of biological transmission , but the gift of God to every man who is born in this world ! Indeed , consciousness could be compared to the light that Jesus puts in every man who is born in this world (John 1: 9). It is the most primitive basis of all morality. It can be suppressed by the negligence or abuse (1 Tim 4 . 2). We must never go against our conscience. Paul did his best to have a " good conscience before God" (Acts 24: 16). What Paul says is that every Christian, in addition to the Holy Spirit, the Spirit of Christ which abides in him, has the conscience which always confirms the testimony of the Holy Spirit and the Word of God (Romans. 9: 1 , 2 Cor 1: 12.) . At the end of this analysis, we will be judged by our response to the realization that God has given us (Rom. 2: 15-16 , 13 : 5). Our conscience can be strong or weak, but more our walk with God , the greater our awareness increases (1 Cor 8 . 7).

10 . THE CHURCH IS THE LIGHT OF THE WORLD

The Lord Jesus used this metaphor when speaking to his disciples in Matthew 5:14 . "You are the light of the world . A city set on a hill can not be hid . " Jesus came to light a fire and the Church is his home. Jesus goes on to say in the same text in verse 16 , " Let your light so shine before men, that they may see your good works, and glorify your Father which is in heaven."
He continues by saying " If you are my disciples , then you are the light of the world. " . Since the Church is the light of the world and the Church of Jesus is divided into Christian communities composed of saints, every believer is **"the light of the world"**. This means that Christian identity is similar to that of God and Jesus by the fact that it is the light . The privilege of being identified with God in this way also has a huge responsibility. It can be summarized as follows : we know properties of the light which should characterize figuratively some important attributes of any Christian.

Christians should be able to light the world; they must be imitators of God (Ephesians 5.1.) As a beloved children , because they came out of the darkness and live in the light (1 John 1:5). And Jesus said , 'You are light. ' By becoming a new creature in Christ , being born again, we are called to be the light and thus to imitate God himself as light.

11 . THE CHURCH IN MISSION

I recall a well-known book entitled " **The City of God** ." This excellent book written by Saint Augustine (354-430) discusses two cities : the City of Man and the City of God. Each has very different characteristics. The city of man is inhabited by a pagan society living according to their passions of the flesh. In contrast, the City of God is composed of true Christians living in accordance with God's will . In this text, St. Augustine meant that the City of God was none other than the Church of God , the assembly of the believers on earth. The hope of Jesus Christ by creating the Church was none other than to create a community of saints diametrically opposed to the sinful human community without God's light.

Jesus said to his disciples and to us today , 'You are this city on the mountain that Isaiah mentioned . This mountain dominates all heights and all peoples is for their salvation . The nations will see that the Lord has established his home on the mountain , in this city, " the City of God", the Church .

12 . THE CHURCH IS DRIVEN BY MEN

The criteria by which those who lead the Church of Jesus Christ are clearly established in the Bible. Paul , who laid the foundations of the Church has left these criteria in his epistles . Those that we find have for generations been applied. Leaders that we admired in our Christian life embodied these criteria. Some are found in I Timothy 3 :1 -13, « Here is a trustworthy saying: Whoever aspires to be an overseer desires a noble task. Now the overseer is to be above reproach, faithful to his wife, temperate, self-controlled, respectable, hospitable, able to teach, not given to drunkenness, not violent but gentle, not quarrelsome, not a lover of money. He must manage his own family well and see that his children obey him, and he must do so in a manner worthy of full[a] respect. (If anyone does not know how to manage his own family, how can he take care of God's church?) He must not be a recent convert, or he may become conceited and fall under the same judgment as the devil. He must also have a good reputation with outsiders, so that he will not fall into disgrace and into the devil's trap.

In the same way, deacons are to be worthy of respect, sincere, not indulging in much wine, and not pursuing dishonest gain. They must keep hold of the deep truths of the faith with a clear conscience. They must first be tested; and then if there is nothing against them, let them serve as deacons.

In the same way, the women[c] are to be worthy of respect, not malicious talkers but temperate and trustworthy in everything.

93

A deacon must be faithful to his wife and must manage his children and his household well. Those who have served well gain an excellent standing and great assurance in their faith in Christ Jesus ».

Deacons must be faithful husbands they assume their responsibilities towards their children and their families . For those who fill out their ministry will have a situation respected and great boldness in the faith in Jesus Christ.

The question of, " who leads the church? " is one of the most important any church community should answer in order to fulfill the mission that Jesus gave to his disciples. To choose church leaders, from the local church to the national level, all decisions on this matter must be taken seriously.

The history of all human institutions shows that the qualification of the leader determines the direction of the institution. We read, for example in the Bible , concerning the history of people of Israel; faithful kings encouraged the people to obey God . The unfaithful ones led the people to disobey God . Leaders are the incarnations of institutions in many ways. Choosing leaders without relying on predefined criteria does more harm than good to the goals and objectives of the institutions and especially to the religious institutions. As far as we are concerned, let us honestly answer this question as active members of our local community churches, are we certain that people we elect in spiritual offices meet recommended criteria according to the Scriptures ? Should we ask why our Churches are what they are ? Here's what Paul said as one of the consequences of such behavior, " For the name of God is blasphemed because of you among the Gentiles , as it is written .

(Romans. 2: 24). It is better to obey God than men as Pierre said in (Acts 4.19) .

Someone wrote these words, *"The church is not built on the talents of a few people but on the sacrifices of all according to the example of Jesus. All are not preachers , but all can spread the fragrance of Christ".* That is where the matter lies . The Church of Jesus Christ is the place where the Spirit of God works. It is this Spirit which has called each member and built his faith in Jesus , and has become saint and a member of his Church in order to perform the work of the Gospel and spread the good news of salvation . Let us defend the message that brought us eternal life. Let us do our best to develop our talents, committing ourselves to work and service for the Church of Jesus Christ on earth.

The Church in all times has always went through difficult periods when man has abused, oppressed and tried to take over . Because of the presence of the Holy Spirit, the Church has always had moments of great awakenings, reforms and revivals . That is why she has been active and alive for the past 2014 years . We remember these atrocities when paganism and corruption took the Church captive in the past . The renewal came with the Reformation of 1514. Let's do our best and the Holy Spirit will do the rest .

13 . JESUS IS THE HEAD OF HIS CHURCH .

At this point in this book, I hear these words of Jesus addressed to Peter echoing , "I tell you that you are Peter, and upon this rock I will build my church, and the gates of Hades shall not prevail against it (Matt.16 : 18). . We know to whom the Church belongs ; we know who died for her; we know who guides and protects her , and we know who is her head. We honor Jesus Christ , the most beloved Son of God. If God allowed Him to leave his throne in heaven and became like us, man through incarnation, to live on earth according to the human conditions without sinning, the one God forsook on the cross just because of our sins , the one who died and rose and is now sited at his Father's right hand, I don't see how his Church will stop being the Church because of man and Satan. God did not allow the Church to cease at the time of 12 apostles , in spite of the persecutions; he did not allow that with Nero and Marcus Aurelius (121-180) ; the Middle Ages (6- 10th c.) and the years inquisitions should have stopped her(15C); the sin of indulgences brought about the Reformation of Martin Luther in 1514. All that did happen during the past 500 years , should have put an end to the Church, but never! Jesus Christ is in control.

There has ALWAYS been in each generation knees that never bended down before the gods of this world. My hope is that you who is reading this book you are and will remain one of those now. The gates of hell shall not prevail against the Church.

14 . PAUL WAS CONCERNED ABOUT THE CHURCH

Paul was very concerned about the future of the Church of Jesus Christ when he was alive and after his death . Listen to his farewell , " Take heed therefore unto yourselves, and to all the flock, over the which the Holy Ghost hath made you overseers, to feed the church of God, which he hath purchased with his own blood. For I know this, that after my departing shall grievous wolves enter in among you, not sparing the flock. Also of your own selves shall men arise, speaking perverse things, to draw away disciples after them. Therefore watch, and remember, that by the space of three years I ceased not to warn every one night and day with tears. And now, brethren, I commend you to God, and to the word of his grace, which is able to build you up, and to give you an inheritance among all them which are sanctified.

". (Acts 20 :28 -32). Paul was a very good pastor ,an educator, and an organizer .

CHAPTER VII

THE APOSTLES' CHURCH

1 . THE DEFINITION OF THE WORD " CHURCH ".

In the Greek language , "church" comes from the preposition " ék " of the source, outside , away from. This preposition denotes separation. It is found in Matthew 2 : 15 .. out of Egypt I called my people. " This means that my people have left Egypt behind . He came out of Egypt. There was more out of this country called Egypt.

The other word which includes the word "church " is " Kaléo " verb meaning to call , as in Matt.20 invite: 8. When evening came , the owner of the vineyard said to his steward , " called the workers ". The direction of calls here means " calls on all workers." Kaléo wants to say that " all call ". We call all those who have the same qualities , the same value, something together. There are similarities. They share a certain identity . Here they are all workers and they will receive the salary of the hands of the same master . Also in Luke 19 : 13. He called ten of his servants. Those he called the group came out of his servants. Those who have been called all his servants. None among them was a non- servant .

The word church in Greek " ekklesia " means meeting a political assembly for example. For the Israelites , had held a meeting for religious purpose) Dt.31 : 30 Judges 20 : 2; For Christians it was the congregation , the church meeting I Cor.11 : 18. The evolution of the name gave rise to the group of Christians living together . Mat.18 : 17 , I Cor. 4: 17; Phil.4 : 15; Act. 15 : 22 . Later this name became the house where believers meet. Rom.16 : 5; cor.16 I : 19. This name has become the universal church I Cor.6 : 4, 12: 28; Eph. 12 : 22 .

2 . AN IMPORTANT REMINDER

We must remember that the church is like those who are called together as Christians , or as a meeting place for those who profess Jesus as their Savior and Lord, either as a universal church, home, family , individuals were the subject of these concepts. Equipment such as construction or organization name had nothing to do with the church name . Those called by God to form the assembly of the saints , as apostles formed the church.

3 . MEMBERSHIP OF THE CHURCH

(1). The church belonged to God .

To the church of God which is at Corinth , to those sanctified in

Christ Jesus I Cor. 1 : 2 . Gal.1 : 13 , I Thess. 1 : 4 ; Act.20 28.

(2) . Jesus is the head of the Church: "God gave him to head throughout the Church which is his body " (Eph. 1: 22)

" It is He, the head of the body, the head of the Church" (Col 1: 18)

3 . It is Jesus who has built His Church . Upon this rock I will build My Church , and the gates of Hades shall not prevail against it . "(Matthew 16:18 b)

(4). Christians form the body of the Church (1 Peter 2:4-9 , 1 Corinthians 3:9-17) " Know ye not that your bodies are members of Christ. ? "(1 Cor 6/15)

"We are all one body in Christ, being members one of another" (Rom 12)

(5). The Church is a congregation of the saints :

To the church of God which is at Corinth , to those sanctified in Christ Jesus I Cor. 1 : 2 . You , on the contrary , you are a chosen race, a royal priesthood, a holy nation , a peculiar people , that you should show forth the praises of him who called you out of darkness into his marvelous light: Which in time past were not a people, but are now the people of God: which had not obtained mercy, but now have obtained mercy . (1 Peter 2.9,10).

CHAPTER VIII

CHRISTIANS' PROBLEMS OF
THE 1st CENTURY

1. THE CHURCH AND THE DEFENDANTS

Jesus, before ascending into heaven to sit at the right hand of the
Father gave this instruction to the eleven disciples , " Go into all the
world and make all nations my disciples " (Matt. 28:19). These last
words of Jesus to the Eleven just before his ascension established
the Church's mission to proclaim the Good News so that will have
the possibility of being saved. The disciples , despite the limitation
of their intellectual capacity, after several years, they put into
writings the life and the ministries of their Master in four Gospels
(Matthew , Mark, Luke and John) . If one left out something very
important in his writing , the other reported it. Because of Jesus
disciples, we have the four Gospels within the New Testament.

The work of the Holy Spirit through the expansion of the
Christian Church was reported to us by Dr. Luke in the book of Acts
. The application and daily living according to the Gospels were

developed by Paul , Peter, James , John and Titus in what we call Epistles and John wrote his famous book of the Revelation. If the Apostles and other leaders of the early Church did not write these 27 books we call the New Testament , we wouldn't have these today.

The Church belongs to Jesus. The Good News the Church announces is the Gospel of Jesus Christ. Officers and all church leaders are called by God to assume the develop, protect, and expend the Church at the same time they should keep it " pure ".

The Church of Jesus must remain the same . The message that we pass on to new generations must remain without corruption. It is our duty to ensure that condition. The enemies of the Church and Jesus' faith doesn't sleep.

2 . THE PERSECUTION

Almost all the 21 epistles written by the apostles were either answers to problems Christian communities were experimenting, prescriptions for proper orders within local churches , exhortations, instructions and warnings against false teachings and bad external influences, recommendations for Christian practical life or reinforcements for the good preparation for the Lord's coming . These epistles have became our prototypes for the Church of Jesus Christ all over the world. The Kingdom of God on earth is built on the same foundations and must win against her enemies .

If one asks many Christians today is the Church persecuted ? We will definitely hear this answer , " No! There is no persecution today . We freely worship our God ".

The objective of the persecution in the early Church was to destroy the Church; to make it disappear. Satan's purpose is still the same today. Anything, or any one who is working against the Church is a persecutor. Jesus said "who is not for us is against us" (Luke 9:50). Saul thought that by killing the disciples and the twelve Apostles, the Gospel of Jesus Christ would disappear and the world would continue as before. When church buildings and temples are getting closed all over , when the number of members from the main denominations keeps decreasing, when theological education is not based on good and true Gospel , when the church does not evangelize , when there is no distinction between those who are Christians and those who are from this world, between Christian and non-Christians, when there is no discipline in the Church, when pastors and priests live as men of the world, when there is no longer distinction between good and evil, should we continue believing that the Church is alive? If killing the disciples and the apostles could have annihilate the Christian faith, what about all those conditions we are living now? If those who belong to the Kingdom of God do not do what the Apostles did in the first century to defend the Church, to teach the pure Gospel, to be aware of the presence of false teachers, to protect the flock of the Lord , to condemn what is not from the Lord and preach the Good News, to equip the saints for the coming at the Lord the danger will still be there. The Church has many persecutors:

Western influence persecutes the Church

Traditions associated with the Gospel persecute the Church .

Paganism persecutes the Church and the Kingdom of Christ.

The indiscipline , the divisions , tribalism, the personal influences , theft , immorality all these elements persecute the Church of Jesus Christ. Should we wait until Jesus we come and speak to us as he did on the road to Damascus ? The same message and question addressed to Saul will be ours,

" WHY ARE YOU PERSECUTING ME? "

We persecute Jesus by persecuting the Church.

We persecute Jesus when working with antichrists .

We persecute Jesus when keeping silence.

We persecute Jesus by turning off our lights from the world.

We will judged if we do nothing !

3 . THE ANTICHISTS

Concerning the antichrists, we will not deal with the OT prophecies or apocalyptical writings of John. I would refer to base my studies on what is said about Christ return based on the Epistles written by the Apostles in the New Testament . The authors of these letters mentioned antichrists .

Here's what John said : " I say this because many deceivers, who do not acknowledge Jesus Christ as coming in the flesh, have gone out into the world. Any such person is the deceiver and the antichrist. [8] Watch out that you do not lose what we[a] have worked for, but that you may be rewarded fully. [9] Anyone who runs ahead and does not continue in the teaching of Christ does not have God; whoever continues in the teaching has both the Father and the Son. If anyone comes to you and does not bring this teaching, do not take them into your house or welcome them. [11] Anyone who welcomes them shares in their wicked work" (II John 1:7-11). Antichrists are deceivers , pure and simple.

The Apostle Paul also warns about false apostles, " For such people are false apostles, deceitful workers, masquerading as apostles of Christ. And no wonder, for Satan himself masquerades as an angel of light. It is not surprising, then, if his servants also masquerade as servants of righteousness. Their end will be what their actions deserve" (II Cor. 11:13-15), which seduced even true Christians to believe in another gospel , follow another Jesus , and bringing another mind, not the mind of God (verses 3-4).

False ministers and false teachers , and false brethren are " tares among the wheat " that Jesus made reference in His parable of Matthew 13 . All these elements work in favor of the spirit of antichrist . They seem sincere , seem spiritual , but it is far from true Christianity . The tares (false ministers and false Christians) are difficult to discern from the wheat (true Christians, those who obey God and are led by the Spirit of the truth). The difficulty of distinguishing the chaff from the wheat makes it easier for False Christians to rise into leadership positions and then infect the church with false doctrines , attractive and disappointing ways. It is unfortunate that they are identified after damages have been done. Thank God! The first century church did a wonderful job and they saved the Truth.

It seems that history repeats itself because we have the same situation today. The Church of Jesus , the Kingdom of God is threatened in every century and at any time. All those who do not preach the pure and true Gospel are called antichrists .

The problem of denying Christ may not be so obvious to everyone. No one of them would say " **I deny Christ."** Notice how Jesus had warned his disciples long ago , "... Watch out that no one deceives you. For many will come in my name, claiming, 'I am the Messiah,' and will deceive many. (Matt. 24:4-5) . The devil is " the god of this world" (II Cor. 4:4) ; he does not want Christians to be prepared for the return of Christ. Here is where we are.

Antichrist may be either an individual, certain teachings , a system, an institution, an ideology , whatever would lead human beings away from Jesus the Savior, whatever is the enemy of the Church is antichrist .

4 . THE CHURCH IN THE HOUSE (oikos)

Christians of the 21st century do not understand that the Church is not the building , an organization, the pastor , but the community based in the family unit. Churches named in the New Testament which the apostles wrote these letters were gathered in individual homes. The home is the first place the Lord should be honored and served.

Joshua proclaimed before the people of Israel, " Me and my

house , we will serve the Lord." Joshua 24:15

When we read the Scriptures , we understand that our home should be a place of piety, of honor, of serve, of love, where members model themselves after the Lord .

The apostles spoke in the New Testament about the church which is " in your house of". Members of that church were, spouses, children , servants and maids . They observed the Word of the Lord. Philemon, Paul's friend , had a church in his house. Philemon 1:2

In these Church homes they broke bread (Acts 2:46) . For the first time in the history of the Church, it was mentioned " discipleship meetings in homes ." It was after Pentecost. Thousands of people believed in the Lord and were baptized when Peter preached that famous sermon at home. Those who believed that day returned to their countries. Those who lived in Mesopotamia, Judea and Cappadocia , Pontus and Asia, Phrygia, Pamphylia , Egypt, the territory of neighboring Libya Cyrene and those who had come from Rome went and brought that Good News at their homes. They returned home carrying in their heart the blessed experience of their new faith in Jesus. They transmitted that Good News to the members of their families. First churches all over the formed in these homes all over the empire.

However the disciples in Jerusalem continued steadfastly going to the temple because they did not understand the difference. Paul and Paul alone understood and created the concept of "CHURCH" " Acts 2:46

A little further we find another reference. " And daily in the temple and at home, they never stopped teaching and proclaiming the good news of Jesus Christ." (Acts 5:42)

After the great persecution that arose with Stephen , the disciples of Jerusalem continued to meet and pray in the houses.

I think we can talk about the first house church in the New Testament , when Cornelius, the Roman centurion received the Lord with all his house .

(Acts 10:48) "And he commanded them to be baptized in the name of the Lord. Then they asked him to stay a few days with them".

The home of Lydia, a seller of purple , was also in the city of Philip in Macedonia , a place where the disciples met . (Acts 16 : 13,16). After his conversion , Lydia put his house at the disposal of the apostles and new converts in the city of Philippi. Aquila and Priscilla , two friends and companions of Paul , gathered a church in their house (Acts 18.26) . The evangelist Philip also attended by disciples with him. (Acts 21:8). The apostle Paul preached and taught in the homes of the disciples (Acts 20:20). In his greetings to the Christians of Rome, the apostle Paul named some home churches (Romans 16:5 , 10, 11); Philemon, Paul's friend had a church in his house. (Phile 1:2)

Here were some benefits of having a church home:
(1) It was a place nearby, avoiding long journeys to visit a remote meeting. (2) One can feel a sense of fellowship, deeper than in an assembly that includes a large number of people , so a better opportunity to practice charity towards each other . (3) It was a great way to reach out with the Gospel people who live nearby. This is a

108

lamp in the house who enlightens all who enter. (Matthew 5.15) .

5 . ENCOURAGEMENT AND ADVICE

The Church today is investing in the construction of buildings we call temples but neglects to prominence for cell of the Church of Christ , the home (oikos) . We see that Paul, whenever he spoke of the application of the Gospel , it included the duties of father , mother , child , servant or slave and neighbor as place of application of Christian teachings. If the house is not the first place to let shine the light we have received from Jesus, if the salt that we are does not season the house, how can we build a city on top of the hill ?

Today's church should be strong at home. Home should be ready to accommodate payer meetings, morning worships , Bible studies etc…. This requires course that there be faithful, humble, willing members to create strong Christian fellowship with others to host others.

I encourage brothers and sisters isolated to hold meetings in their homes. The Lord has promised his presence where two or three are gathered in his name. What is important is to gather in his name and he will lead.

Pray that our homes become places of prayer and spiritual meetings , without being cut from Christian Community Center to which we belong .

There's still a lot to say, but I simply wanted to give you my views on home churches. We all need edification in Christ through the Holy Spirit and according to His Holy Word. .

CHRISTIANS' ATTRIBUTES.

I chose a few verses from the Bible and especially the epistles to emphasize the importance of these 21 letters in the lives of those who are saved . Analyze, preach, study to understand these verses for your own benefit as a Christian. They provide in depth a summary of this book.

I Peter 3:15

1 . Christians honor Christ in his heart .

2 . There is hope

3 . He is generous and respectful **Galatians 5:22**

4 . Produce the fruit of the Spirit is love, joy, peace, patience, kindness, goodness , faithfulness, **1 Peter 3:02**

5 . It has a pure conduct. **2 Timothy 3:16-17**

6 . He believes that All Scripture is inspired by God and profitable for teaching, for reproof, for correction , for instruction in righteousness, that the man of God may be competent , equipped for every good work. **James 1:5**

7 . He asked and obtained his wisdom, God, **2 Timothy 3:15** He believes that the Bible will make him wise unto salvation through faith in Jesus Christ **1 Corinthians 13:1-13**

8 . He believes and practices the love of God **1 John 5:3**

9 . It keeps the commandments of God . **1 John 3:6**

10 . He believes that anyone who lives in God does not continue to

sin ; someone who sins has not seen or experienced God.**1 Corinthians 2:37**

11 . To be spiritual , we must recognize what is written in the Bible

as the Lord's commandment . **Romans 8:02**

12 . The Christian believes that the law of the Spirit of life has freed him in Christ Jesus from the law of sin and death. **Romans 4:1-25**

13 . He believes in God. His work is considered as a gift and due to God. He is justified by faith and becomes just in the blood of Christ. **John 20:31**

14 . He believes that Jesus is the Christ , the Son of God, and that believing you may have life in his name. **John 14:21**

15 .He believes God's commands is a proof that we love .**Matt 5:48**

16 . He must be perfect as his heavenly Father is perfect .

   1 John 4:18

16. He believes that perfect love casts out fear . Fear related to punishment , and whoever fears has not been perfected in love . **1 John 2:1**

17 . He knows he should not sin. But if he manages to sin , he has an advocate with the Father , Jesus Christ the righteous . **1 John 1:7**

18 . He knows that if he walks in the light as God is in the light, he has fellowship with one another, and the blood of Jesus his Son cleanses him from all sin. **1 John 1:3-4**

19 . He knows that believing and living by the Word of God , he will be in communion with other Christians, with the Father and with his Son Jesus Christ. **James 5:16**

20 . He believes that Christians should confess their sins to one another , and pray one for another , so they can be healed. The prayer of a righteous great power. **James 1:22**

21 . He believes he must not only listen to the Word, but he must implement it , do what he says . **Hebrews 11:1**

22 . He believes that faith is the assurance of things hoped for , the evidence of things not seen. **Hebrews 6:1-20**

23 . He believes he must grow in his Christian life to wait for maturity, until the resurrection of the dead, and of eternal judgment , to do what God allows . For it is impossible , in the case of those who have once been enlightened , who have tasted the heavenly gift, and have shared the Holy Spirit , and have tasted the good word of God and the powers of the age to come, to be lost. **1 Timothy 3:15**

24. He knows how to behave in the house of God, which is the church of the living God , a pillar and buttress of the truth. **2 Corinthians 11:1-33**

25 . He knows he must be careful not to be deceived, but to have a sincere and pure devotion to Christ. Do not accept a gospel other than the one who brought him salvation in Christ. **1 Cor. 2:14**

26 . He believes that physical man received not the things of the Spirit of God: for they are foolishness to him, and he is not able to understand because it is only spirit that can judge . **John 14:6**

27 . He believes that Jesus is the way and the truth and the life . No one comes to the Father except through him. **Matthew 5:1-48**

28 . He believes that the poor in spirit are blessed because, for theirs is the kingdom of heaven, blessed are those who mourn for they \

shall be comforted. Blessed are the meek for they shall inherit the earth as Jesus said.

Ecclesiastes 24:14

29 . He believes that God will bring every work into judgment, with every secret thing , whether good or evil. **1 John 3:1-24**

30 . Because God loved us and that is why we are called the children of God . For this reason, we are not recognized by the world. Therefore, all those who hope in him purify themselves even as he is pure. Everyone who practices sin also practices lawlessness . **1 John 1:8**

31. He knows that if he says he has no sin, he deceives himself and the truth is not in him . **1 Peter 1:7**

32 . He knows and believes that when faith is tested , it is more precious than gold that perishes though it is tested by fire, which result in praise , glory and honor at the revelation of Jesus Christ. **1 Peter 1:5**

33 . That believers are guarded through faith in the power of God unto salvation ready to be revealed in the last time . **1 Thess 5:23**

34 . He thinks he can be completely sanctified by the peace of God, and the whole spirit , soul and body may be preserved blameless at the coming of our Lord Jesus Christ.**1 Thessalonians 4:03**

35 . He believes that his sanctification is the will of God , he must abstain from sin. **Ephesians 4:13**

36 . He must grow in the Christian life to reach full spiritual maturity , to the measure of the stature of the fullness of Christ, **Eph. 2:8-9**

37 . He is saved by grace through faith in Jesus Christ. And it is not by himself, it is the gift of God, not of works, lest any man should

boast.

Galatians 6:04

38 . He knows and believes he must test his own work. **Gal. 6:2**

39 . He must bear the burdens of others , as others carry his own, in order to fulfill the law of Christ. (The law of love) **Galatians 5:05**

40 . He looked forward to by faith in the Spirit for the hope of righteousness **Galatians 5:1**

41 . He believes that the freedom of Christ was released, and it must stand firm and do not submit again to a yoke of slavery .

 (Sin , Satan, the flesh, the world) **2 Corinthians 7:01**

42 . He believes that the Christian must be purified from all filthiness of the flesh and spirit , which brings holiness to the end in the fear of God.

2 Corinthians 4:18

43 . He believes that he should not look to visible things, but the things that are unseen . For the things which are seen are transient , but the things that are unseen are eternal. **1 Corinthians 12:1-31**

44 . He believes that there are diversities of gifts, but the same Spirit , and there are varieties of service, but the same Lord ; **1**

Corinthians 2:16

45 . He must believe firmly that he has the Spirit of Christ. **1 Cor. 2:1-16**

46 . He must admit that his faith is based not on human wisdom but on the power of God. **1 Corinthians 1:10**

47 . He must do all that there is no division between Christ , but the unit in the same mind and the same judgment. **Romans 12:2**

48 . He should never conform to this world but be transformed by

the renewing of his mind, by the testes , it may discern what is the will of God, what is good and acceptable and perfect . **Romans 12:1**

49 . The Christian must present his body to God as a living sacrifice, holy and acceptable , which is her spiritual worship. **Romans 8:28**

50 . Because he loves God, the Christian must know that God loves so will ensure that all things work together for the good because it is called according to God's plan . **Romans 6:22**

51 . Christians must firmly believe that he was free from sin and became the slave of God and therefore the fruit it bears God is sanctification to eternal life . **Romans 6:06**

52 . He knows he is aware that his old man was crucified with Christ, so that the body of sin might be nullified , so that it would no longer be enslaved to sin. **Romans 5:12**

53. He knows and believes and understands that , just as sin entered the world through one man, and death through sin, and so death spread to all men because all sinned - **Romans 3:23**

54 . He knows , he believes and understands that all have sinned and come short of the glory of God **Acts 3:23**

55 . He knows , he believes and understands that every soul that does not listen to the Word of God must be destroyed. **Acts 2:38**

56 . He knows , he believes and understands that every sinner must repent and be baptized in the name of Jesus Christ for the forgiveness of his sins , he will receive the Holy Spirit.

116

THE CHRISTIANS' CHARACTERISTICS

Dr. Richard J. Krejcir wrote an article in which he gives a long list of some attributes that describe the spiritual fruit that produces the actual divine relationship and engagement with the Christian Spirit, Christ and His Word . This list is the fiber of our moral center that goes into all our character throughout our existence kissing and holding all our relationships when it is sealed as a choice. The effects of this list are stronger than our feelings.

Anyone who has incarnated in this list takes his character 's real name Christian. This list and other characteristics that are similar identify those who belong to the Kingdom of God on this earth.

(1) Those in this group identify with John the Baptist recognized that it is Christ who must be cared for while , he must lower , decrease (Jon 3:29-30) . If we refuse this vital call, the work of the Church of Jesus will be problems and risk of falling (1 Cor 1:30 ; Col 1:27, 1 Thess 4:03 ;5:23-24 ; 1 Peter 1:5) . .

(2) Galatians gives us the fruit of the Spirit (Galatians 5:22-23) . A fruit consists of several sections inside .

The fruit of Galatians in Galatians 5:22-23 . -

The love. (John 13:1 ; 3:13 p.m. ; 1 Corinthians 1:03 p.m.)

Joy . (Proverbs 3:13 p.m. , John 15:11 ; 5:13 p.m.)

Peace. (Matthew 5:9 , Colossians 3:15 , Philippians 4:07)

117

Patience is tolerant . (Matthew 27:14 , Romans 12:12 ; Jacques 1:3,12)

Kindness is kindness practice. (Ephesians 4:32)

 Pleasures . (Matthew 19:16)

Faithfulness (Matthew 5:19 p.m. , 25:21 , 1 Cor 12:9 ; . Heb.11:1)

Sweetness (Phil 4: .. 5 2 Timothy 2:24 , 1 Thess 2:07)

Auto- control (1 Thessalonians 5 , 22). Forgiveness . (Luke 23:34 , Ephesians 4:32 , Colossians 3:13)

Humility (Luke 22:27 ; . Phil 2:08 , 1 Peter 5:3-5)

The fairness , **equal**, even if it hurts us . (Matthew 7:12)

Courage realizes the danger .. (Deut. 31:6 , 1 John 4:4)

Friendship (Proverbs 27:17)

Honesty , Truth, right. (2 Cor 8:21 ; . Ephesians 4:25)

Reliable and trustworthy. (1 Cor 4:2; . Colossians 1:10)

Gratitude . (1 Corinthians 4:07 , 1 Thessalonians 5: 18).

Be responsible , know and do. (Romans 14:12)

Contentment. (Romans 9:19-21 ; Phil 4: 10-13 , 1 Tim 6:6-9) .

Generosity. (Deut. 4:17 p.m. ; Matthew 10:8)

Purity and Holiness . (Matt. 5:08 , Phil 4:8 , 1 Tim 1:5 . 4:8 James 4:13) **Confidence** (Philippians .

Encouragement . (Ps.119 : 28; Matt 3:17 ; 1Thess 5:11-14)

Availability ready to adjust its schedule. (Mc1 :17 -18 , Acts 16:10)

The **Listening** (Hebrews 2:01)

Wisdom truly desires knowledge (1 Kings 3:09 ; Ps119 :97 -98)

Compassion. (Job 29:13 ; Luke 1:41 ET 7:04 p.m. ; 1 Peter 3:8)

Enthusiasm (Matt : 5:16 , Rom 12:11 , Gal 6:09 , Col 3:23 .) .

Initiative. (Prov. 10:29 p.m. , Philippians 3:14 , 4:13-15)

Stagecoach (Prov. 10:04 ; . Rom 24:11 , Colossians 3:23)

Being Truthful (Philippians 2:4)

Efficiency (Psalm 90:12 ; 4:23 ephemeral ; 5:15 - 16 , 1 Pet.4:10) .

Discretion . (Ps.112 : 5; Prov. 22:3 ; Rom.12 : 2, 9 , 2:19 p.m. , 22)

Optimism . (Luke 9:18 p.m. , John 16:33 , Romans 8:25 , 28)

Obedience (Deut. 13 . John 14:14 ; 3:14 p.m. 2 Corinthians 10:05)
(1 Peter 2:13-14)

Being Nice . (Amos 3:3)

The Rating (Romans 12:10)

Avoid anger. (Jacques 1:19)

Be a good example (1 Peter 2:21-2 ; 1 Peter 2:12,15,17)

Child Faith (Mt 18:2-4 , 34)

Commitment is dedicated (1 Timothy 6:20)

Learn Communicate . (1 Timothy 4:12)

Conviction . (Daniel 1:08)

Cooperation (Eph. 4:3)

Creativity be resourceful and imaginative. (1 Timothy 4:14)

The Diligent . (Colossians 3:23)

The dependability . (Psalm 119:30 ; 2 Timothy 4:7,8)

Deference is to be ready to fold freedom. (Romans 2:21 p.m.)

Devotional be aligned. (Colossians 3:02)

Discernment is the ability to see people and situations as they are (
1 Samuel 4:07 p.m. , 7:02 p.m. Proverbs)

Being Diplomatic is the ability to not be intimidated. (Psa 112:5)

No defamation refuses to hurt others ! (Jacques 1:26)

The endurance , inner strength (Galatians 6:09) A healthy mind e .
(2 Timothy 1:7)

Flexibility. (Colossians 3:02)

Piles. (Matthew 6:33)

Godliness is to be pious . (3 John 11)

Grace is an elegant simplicity and calm that minimizes .

Harmless. (Hebrews 7:26)

Honest is to be sincere . (Hebrews 7:26)

Hospitality is a willingness to share . (Romans 24:13)

Integrity is obedience to a moral code of values (Ps78 : 72)

Loyalty remain attached . (Proverbs 17:17)

The sweetness is not to be weak ! . (Psalms 62:5)

Show more merciful indulgence (Luke 6:36) Perseverance is not
low. (Galatians 6:9)

Persuasion calls the Word of God. (2 Timothy 2:25)

Being Prompt (Ecclesiastes 3:1)

Prudence, logical and fair judgment. (Prove. 1:06 p.m. , 10:3.)

Security is trust. (Proverbs 29:25 , John 6:27)

Get Submitted is with fear and respect. (Ephesians 5:21)

Self-acceptance is the realization (2 Corinthians 12:9-10)

Altruism is the gift . (Titus 2:14)

Sensitivity (Romans 12:15)

Servant Leadership . (Luke 10:26 p.m.)

Sincerity (Joshua 24:14 , 1 Peter 1:22)

Success (Matthew 25:21)

Support (Galatians 6:2)

Tact and diplomacy (Colossians 4:06)

Teaching (Matt.7 : 28 , John 7:16 , Mark 4:02 , 2 John 1:9)

Tolerant is to be lenient (1 Thess. 5:14)

Rigor. (Ecclesiastes 9:10 , Colossians 3:23)

Understanding is the ability to reason (Psalm 119:34)

Virtue principles of moral excellence (Col. 3:12-17)

Zealous enthusiasm. (Luke 2:49 , John 2:17 8:29)

There are more than 60 characters complete studies on the departments website http://www.discipleshiptools.org/ to our character and http://www.intothyword.org/ on Canal Bible studies.

© 2002 RJ Krejcir in your Word Ministries

http://www.discipleshiptools.org/

Richard Joseph Krejcir is the Director of 'Into Thy Word Ministries , " a ministry of discipleship . He is the author of the book, in your Word and is also a pastor, teacher, lecturer and a graduate of Fuller Theological Seminary in Pasadena, California .

Are there a love , joy , peace, patience, kindness, goodness , faithfulness, gentleness and self-control in your parish or church? How would you describe your leadership? How to have the majority of Christians do you know? Are there a difference between leaders and Christians you know and those who are not Christians ? If yes, what are the differences ? If not, why ?

The lust of the flesh

If you liked this book , recommend it to other Christians. You can get " Amazon.fr . "

BIOGRAPHY

1 . Second the Bible in French

2 . Hearing God: Developing a Conversational Relationship with God ,

   by Dallas Willard 1984

3 . Spirituality According To Paul , Imitating the Apostle of Christ,

   by Rodney Reeves, 1957

4 . Donald Guthrie . New Testament Theology . InterVarsity , 1981.

   "The Mission of Christ, " pages 408-509 .

5 . George Eldon Ladd . The Theology of the New Testament. Eerdmans , 1993.

   " Paul , " pages 397-614 .

6 . David Wenham . Paul : Follower of Jesus or Founder of Christianity ?

   Eerdmans , 1995. Often technical .

7 . The Life and Letters of Paul the Apostle, by Lymon Abbott,

Made in the USA
Charleston, SC
26 January 2014